365 Games smart babies play

Playing, Growing and Exploring with Babies from Birth to 15 Months

2nd Edition

Sheila Ellison and Susan Ferdinandi

SOURCEBOOKS, INC.®
NAPERVILLE, ILLINOIS

This publication is designed to provide accurate and authoritative information in regard to the subject matter covered. It is sold with the understanding that the publisher is not engaged in rendering legal, accounting, or other professional service. If legal advice or other expert assistance is required, the services of a competent professional person should be sought.
—From a Declaration of Principles Jointly Adopted by a Committee of the American Bar Association and a Committee of Publishers and Associations

All brand names and product names used in this book are trademarks, registered trademarks, or trade names of their respective holders. Sourcebooks, Inc., is not associated with any product or vendor in this book.

Published by Sourcebooks, Inc.
P.O. Box 4410, Naperville, Illinois 60567-4410
(630) 961-3900
FAX: (630) 961-2168
www.sourcebooks.com

Originally published in 2003

The Library of Congress has catalogued the first edition as follows:
Ellison, Sheila.
365 games babies play / by Sheila Ellison and Susan Ferdinandi.
   p. cm.
ISBN 1-4022-0536-8 (alk. paper)
1. Infants—Miscellanea. 2. Infants—Care—Miscellanea. 3. Parenting—Miscellanea.
4. Play—Miscellanea. 5. Creative activities and seat work—Miscellanea.
I. Ferdinandi, Susan. II. Title.
HQ774.E485   2003
649'.122—dc20   200333707

Printed and bound in the United States of America
VHG   10   9   8   7   6   5   4   3   2   1

Acknowledgments

To Lauren Zimet, M.S., CCC/SLP Speech Language Pathologist, and Robin J. Skolsky, MSPT, Physical Therapist, for contributing activity ideas as well as enthusiastic professional guidance in the areas of development, language, and the physical needs of babies.

To my children Wesley, Brooke, Rhett, and Troy for teaching me how to love unconditionally, and to my parents Nancy and Dave Maley for all their "Grandparenting" time.

—Sheila

To my sister and co-author Sheila Ellison for her generous encouragement and guidance throughout the writing of this book.

—Susan

Dedication

To my twelve-year-old son, Troy, for teaching me
that any difficulty can be overcome.
For inspiring me each day with his courage, determination,
and willingness to live life to its fullest,
even when it's a challenge.

—Sheila Ellison

To my husband Dale and my children Dillon and Elizabeth.
Thank you for all the baby days.

—Susan Ferdinandi

Introduction

We believe that the magic of childhood lies in the everyday moments. From birth through two years old, most moments are spent caring for, teaching, holding, and growing through baby's first experiences. There are so many things baby learns to do in such a short time that sometimes we blink and a stage is gone. This book will give you ideas of ways to spend magical time together. Included are sections on floor time, language and sound, nature, art, music, movement, family growth, grandparenting, parks and recreation, water play, siblings, and storytelling.

Each section starts with infant-appropriate activities and progresses up through about fifteen months. Since age doesn't dictate ability, try things out and see what your baby likes and can do. The best way for you to understand your baby is to observe, so pay attention to baby's growing personality. Babies bring joy, they teach life. What a wonderful gift!

Sheila Ellison   Susan Ferdinandi

Wit & Wisdom

The advice in the Wit & Wisdom sections of this book was given to us by parents from across the country who wanted to pass on their tricks, tips, baby secrets, and wisdom to you. We would like to thank them for sharing their experiences with us. We're always looking for good advice to be added to future editions, so write to us care of Sourcebooks or visit Sheila Ellison at www.CompleteMom.com.

Table of Contents

Baby's Room

Floortime

Movement

Art and Sculpture

On the Go

Child Care/Playgroups

Parks, Playgrounds, and Outdoor Play

Celebrations

Family Growth

caregiving

bonding

Ages: 0 to 3 months

What bonding is, or can be for you and baby, is time spent listening, looking, touching, talking, holding, stroking, cuddling, playing, and singing together. It is sending baby a clear message, by your actions, that you care deeply and can be counted on. Some of your greatest opportunities for bonding occur when caring for baby's needs. These needs fill much of your time together in the form of feeding, diapering, napping, bathing, and dressing. They provide regular times for you and baby to be close and learn from each other. Take ten minutes right now to visualize the kind of relationship you desire to have with baby as he or she grows up.

diaper time!

Ages: 0 to 3 months

Include baby while diapering by talking about what you are doing. Talk to baby about what is going on, and mention the parts of baby's body as you touch them. Here are some ways to involve baby: say, "I'm going to change your diaper," "Here is your wet diaper," "You help me when you hold still." Diapering is a perfect time to gently massage baby's foot, stomach, back, face, or hands. It is also a good time to say rhymes or sing songs. You may also want to touch or rub baby's skin with various textures like a feather, piece of velvet, sheepskin, or silk scarf. Or buy a small, colorful beach ball and roll it up and down baby's tummy. Hang a secure, safe mirror alongside the changing table so baby has a good view when being changed.

★ Wit & Wisdom ★

Many new moms are back to using cloth diapers and rubber pants. To keep rubber pants soft, add vegetable oil to the wash.
—Beth, Alton, Illinois

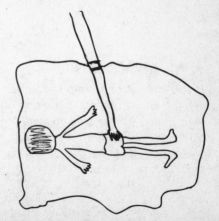

2

bottle- or breast-feeding

Ages: 0 and up

Whether baby is nursed, bottle-fed, or both, feeding times are precious because of the physical closeness and warmth you share. Baby will study your face very carefully, seeking eye contact with you. It's better to relax and drink in that shining face than to sit calculating how many ounces baby has consumed. If you are bottle-feeding, hold the bottle close to your body to encourage baby to look up at your face. Do this little relaxation exercise while you are nursing: starting with your toes, tense the muscle then relax, move up your body tensing every muscle for a few seconds then consciously relaxing it. (This is also a great exercise to do before bed if you have a hard time falling asleep.)

★ Wit & Wisdom ★

If you are getting confused which breast you fed baby from last, put a ring on one of your fingers on the side you will feed baby from next. Switch it after you feed.
—Elizabeth P., Jacksonville, Florida

3

mama's scent

Ages: 0 to 12 months

Keep a burp cloth or blanket on you, especially when you are nursing. The scent of your milk, your skin, and of baby will seep into the fabric and can provide comfort when another caretaker is with baby. When baby is young, loose blankets or pillows are not recommended in a crib or bassinet unless tightly swaddled, so don't leave this cloth with baby unsupervised.

4

★ **Wit & Wisdom** ★

When my baby was little I would put him in a front pack while I did household chores like sweeping, dishes, raking leaves, or cooking. He loved being snuggled close and I loved getting a few things done.
—Margie S., Portland, Oregon

baby's right to cry

Ages: o and up

Baby's cry can evoke a wide range of feelings in those who hear it: worry, fear, frustration, anger, and sadness. When baby cries, try your best to find out why by listening, looking, and feeling for the answer. Once you've exhausted all the possibilities—wet, hungry, hot, cold, bored, tired, lonely, feverish, or other visible physical symptoms (and called your pediatrician if you believe the problem is medical)—you've done your best. You will not always discover why baby is crying, and that's OK. Ask baby why he or she is crying and leave space for baby to respond. Setting up this two-way communication even before baby speaks recognizable words is very important, establishing a healthful pattern for your growing relationship. When baby cries and you don't understand why, hold baby, or place baby in a crib, or on a cozy blanket on the floor. Close your eyes, take several deep breaths, exhaling slowly, and remember that crying is part of being alive and being human; it is also baby's unique form of communication.

safe to explore

Ages: 3 months and up

Although movement is limited during the first few months of life, it is still possible for babies to wiggle and turn themselves into potential danger. Check all areas of a room baby might be able to squirm, wiggle, roll, or scoot to. Never leave baby on a high surface alone. Get down on the floor and check for things that baby could pull on, crawl into, crawl under, chew and swallow, squeeze, or throw.

- Cover electrical outlets and all heaters.
- Protect baby from windows and mirrors that are not shatterproof.
- Tie up all drapery cords or any kind of string.
- Get rid of slippery throw rugs and poisonous plants.
- Cribs and other furniture for baby must meet consumer-protection safety standards. Crib mattress must fit snugly so baby can't get stuck between the mattress and side of the crib and smother.
- Keep all medicines and cleaning materials out of baby's reach.
- Allow no toys with small parts that can come off and be swallowed by baby.
- Make sure all toys and materials are nontoxic.
- Babyproof cupboards containing sharp, poisonous, or breakable objects.
- Move or stabilize furniture, like bookshelves, that baby could knock over.
- Keep a first-aid kit and know CPR.
- Make sure emergency phone numbers are by the phone.

daily routine

Ages: 3 months and up

Babies love routine. If you can get some sort of routine going, your life will be easier, and baby will know what to expect. More important, you will have a plan. It is a good idea to build your daily routing around what baby already does. For the next three days, write down when baby eats and sleeps. After a few days, you will see a pattern developing. Decide on a time close to baby's patterned time and follow through for a week eating or sleeping at that time. This gives you time to schedule your own life, creating a calmer and more assured parent. This daily routine will also make it easier for other caretakers to care for your baby.

look before you leap

Ages: 6 months and up

Look before you leap into solving baby's dilemmas (unless the situation is dangerous), and identify what baby is trying to do. Support and encourage baby's effort, but allow baby to do what he or she is capable of doing. Help with tasks that prove too frustrating. One situation might be that baby crawls under a coffee table and starts to cry. Instead of running over and pulling baby out, involve baby by lying down on the floor and talking about the situation; "I see you're stuck under here," then gently guide baby out. Episodes like this will happen often and are real learning experiences in problem-solving.

8

★ Wit & Wisdom ★

When you take baby from the crib or cradle in the middle of the night, place a heating pad in the empty crib so when the feeding is over, baby can return to a warm, cozy bed.
—Elaine W., Boston, Massachusetts

when baby grabs the spoon

Ages: 6 to 12 months

Take it as a sign that they want to feed themselves, or at least try! Here are some ideas to help make this transition successful.

- Use unbreakable, child-sized utensils. In the beginning, offer another spoon for baby to hold while you feed him or her.
- Offer finger food—small pieces of soft food that baby can pick up, such as bananas.
- Small quantities of food are better than overwhelming baby with "family style" servings. Baby can always have more and there won't be so much mess to clean up.
- Self-feeding is most successful in a relaxed atmosphere. There is nothing like having your face wiped every time cereal drops on your chin to take the fun out of eating.
- When baby stops eating, end the meal and clear baby's place, unless you want to see whatever is left smeared over everything within reach.

★ Wit & Wisdom ★

When my son Julian was beginning to eat, I would put a standing mirror in front of him so he could see himself. He loved watching himself eat and I think he learned more quickly how to hold the spoon.
—Gail, Key West, Florida

the gift of gab

Ages: 9 months and up

Oh, how thrilling to hear baby's words come trickling out—first one word, then three, followed by two- and three- word sentences! Now more than ever, speak clearly and directly to baby. Use fewer words such as, "let's wash hands, it's dinner time," instead of, "It's time to wash your hands because we're going to be eating dinner in about five minutes." When baby talks to you respond and add to what was said. Baby might say, "Daddy eat," and you repeat, "yes, Daddy is going to eat" or "Daddy will eat with us."

★ **Wit & Wisdom** ★

When my daughter was just weeks old, I would talk to her constantly, giving her a play-by-play narrative of whatever I was doing. She would lie in her cradle nearby and I'd chat while I set the table, unloaded the dishwasher, or put groceries away.
—Lauren Z., Atlanta, Georgia

bathroom exploration

Ages: 12 months and up

Spend some time exploring the bathroom with baby. Show how different objects found in the bathroom are used. Show baby how they work together, like a toothbrush and toothpaste, hairbrush and hair, sponge and soap, etc. Wet baby's hands and dry them with a towel. Fill up the bathtub a little and talk about how the drain holds water in, then lets it out. Flush the toilet a few times. Remember, even if baby is not able to ask questions, he or she is still wondering.

★ **Wit & Wisdom** ★

As baby begins to use the toilet, use baby wipes instead of toilet paper.
—Howard V., Exeter, New Hampshire

11

getting dressed

Ages: 18 months and up

While you are getting dressed, have a little fun teaching baby the names of clothes: socks, shoes, T-shirt, pants, sweatshirt, dress. Put two articles of clothing out on the floor next to baby and say, "Baby touch the (clothing)." Wait a minute for baby to respond, then say, "Let's put the (clothing) on!" Replace the article of clothing with another and repeat until baby is dressed. You could also trace your child on a large piece of butcher paper, and have baby lay out her clothes on top of the paper person—a great way to pick out clothes to wear for the next day.

★ **Wit & Wisdom** ★

Amanda loved our dressing game each morning. I would put each piece of clothing on halfway, then let her finish it up. She liked being a team, and I think she was satisfied that she was doing part of it herself.
—Susan K., Cedarburg, Wisconsin

12

make a potty book

Ages: 18 to 24 months

Make a book titled *Bye Bye Diapers, Hello Potty*. Write a short story about your child and any imaginary-character friends. The story should be about how they learn to use the toilet like a big boy or girl. Most children love to hear stories about themselves. Make sure to incorporate positive reinforcement strategies you use at home into the book so baby can see the reward in using the toilet.

13

★ Wit & Wisdom ★

Put several drops of either red, green, or blue food coloring in the potty before they go. They will be so excited to see it change color that they will look forward to doing it again.

—Dawn P., West Palm Beach, Florida

beginning of language

tippy toe

Ages: 0 and up

Tippy Tippy Tiptoe, off we go.
Tippy Tippy Tiptoe, to and fro.
Tippy Tippy Tiptoe, through the house.
Tippy Tippy Tiptoe, quiet as a mouse.

Use your fingers to "tiptoe" up baby's arm, over his or her head, and down the other arm. Tiptoeing around the house while holding baby and whispering the words is another way for baby to experience your voice. If you're both walking, baby might enjoy leading you around as you say the rhyme together.

gurgles and coos

Ages: 3 to 6 months

Conversation with your baby can begin at birth. By three to six months, baby will begin making babbling sounds. When baby makes these sounds, make similar sounds back and look into baby's eyes and smile. As baby grows, the ability to vocalize new sounds increases, especially if they have been spoken and sung to by a sensitive caregiver. When baby engages you in conversation by making sounds, begin repeating the sound back to baby as it might be contained in a familiar word. For example, baby says "pa", and you say "Papa", ba...bottle, ma...mama, be...baby, and so on. Older siblings are good at coming up with creative words. Baby reaches out in many ways to communicate. Paying attention and responding encourages language development.

15

★ Wit & Wisdom ★

Every stuffed animal my daughter received as a gift was named using the last name of the person who gave it to her. She now has a lasting relationship with these people through her animal friends.
—Mary Jane W., Grafton, Wisconsin

baby sign

Ages: 3 months and up

Research indicates that children benefit from the use of signs and gestures to enhance communication and decrease frustration. Begin signing with your baby at birth. Make up hand gestures for everyday words and actions like, "eat," "drink," "sleep," "play," etc. Whenever you say that word, use a hand signal to go along with it. Teach these hand signals to baby's brothers and sisters. One aspect of new babies that frustrates siblings is their lack of communication skills. This might be an interesting experiment to help the older child connect with baby.

There are many books on this topic if you would like to learn more. My favorite is *Baby Signs*, by Linda Acredolo and Susan Goodwyn.

★ Wit & Wisdom ★

When my daughter Brooke was 9 months old, she woke up one night crying…I was walking with her, rocking, singing, anything to calm her down, when all of a sudden she signed "drink!" It was totally amazing.
—Lauren Z., Atlanta, Georgia

baker's baby

Ages: 6 to 12 months

Set baby on your lap facing you. As you hold baby's hands, gently make that cake together.

> *Pat-a-cake, pat-a-cake baker's man*
> *(clap hands together)*
> *Bake me a cake as fast as you can*
> *Roll 'em and roll 'em and mark 'em with a B*
> *(roll hands around and trace letter on baby's hand)*
> *And toss 'em in the oven for baby and me.*
> *(point to baby, then yourself)*

Lie baby on back and repeat using baby's feet. Repeat this many times if baby approves.

more piggy toes

Ages: 6 to 12 months

Here's a chance to play with those adorable, tiny feet. Hold baby's big toe gently between your thumb and index finger and say:

This little piggy went to market. (big toe)
This little piggy stayed home. (second toe)
This little piggy had roast beef. (third toe, eggplant may be substituted for vegetarians)
This little piggy had none. (fourth toe)
This little piggy cried wee, wee, wee all the way home. (fifth toe)

As you say "wee, wee, wee," walk fingers up baby's leg, across tummy, and up to chin and lightly tickle.

★ Wit & Wisdom ★

I found a great way to wash stuffed animals. Load a pillowcase with the dirty stuffed animals, tie it closed, and put it through the wash and dry cycles. The animals will come out fluffy and new.
—Jill S., Oxnard, California

instant replay

Ages: 6 to 12 months

Materials
Tape recorder
Blank cassette tape

Record baby's sounds and the conversations you have together. Play them back and observe baby's response. Some babies become quite animated and vocalize, while others become quite still. Older babies may want to push the buttons of the recorder. Have fun with this, and remember, most recorders are built to withstand the pressure of curious little hands.

19

★ **Wit & Wisdom** ★

My kids love sand. I found that a little cornstarch on a piece of cloth is a gentle way of rubbing off all the sand from hands and feet before climbing into a clean car, or marching into the house.
—Holly S., Minnetonka, Minnesota

picture this

Materials
Magazines, picture books, catalogs

Sit with baby on your lap. As you turn the pages of the book or magazine, point out and name objects baby might recognize. Say things like, "See the baby," "Look at the dog," "The bike is red." You may also want to encourage baby to point to the pictures you are naming. Begin this by saying "Touch _____" and model the touching or pointing to the pictures you are naming. Initially, just model this for baby. Later you can assist baby by moving his or her hand to the picture you named. Baby can also learn how to turn the page. Chunky cardboard pages work best for this. Simply say, "turn page," and help baby to turn the page.

put in—take out

Ages: 6 to 12 months

Materials
Colorful pop-beads, large plastic toys or any safe item for baby to handle, large plastic or wooden bowl or container

Give one of the toy items to baby and say, "put in," and have him or her put it in the bowl. Repeat this action a dozen times. Play this game daily and soon baby will learn the words "put in." After baby appears to understand what it means to put a toy in, demonstrate the words "take out." This concept is harder to master, so you may have to guide baby's hand. Lastly you can teach "give me please." Baby holds the container of items and you hold out your hand to request one. Make sure to praise baby throughout this activity. By modeling language for baby, she will begin to learn pronouns ("he," "she," "him," "her") from hearing you talk.

nose, eyes, hands

Ages: 6 to 12 months

Pick one body part to focus on for an entire day, such as hands. Sing songs about hands, point hands out in storybooks, on people, pets, television, etc. Take baby on a walk around the house, pointing to hands wherever you see them. Wiggle, wave, clap, or shake your hands. Do the same for nose, ears, feet, etc., using the following ideas: breathe through your nose and let baby feel the air or hum and let baby feel your nose vibrate; listen to each other's heartbeat; dance with your feet, or lie on your backs and wiggle them in the air; talk about or make noises with your teeth, tongue, and lips, blow air out, whistle, make popping sounds with your lips, open and close your mouth. The options are endless, so have fun.

22

uh-oh, it's the giant

Ages: 9 to 12 months

These two action rhymes are fun to do when baby has begun to babble long and short groups of sounds, such as tatata, bibibi, dada, etc. They are short, repetitive, and include several sounds already, or soon to be, in baby's repertoire. Exposing baby to rhyming words, poetry, and nursery rhymes is great for early language development.

> *Fee Fi Fo Fum—Here's my fingers, here's my thumb.*
> (wave fingers, then thumb)
> *Fee Fi Fo Fum—Fingers gone, so is thumb.*
> (curl four fingers into fist, then thumb follows)

Repeat this replacing the letter *F* in "Fee Fi Fo Fum" with the letters *B*, *T*, *D*, and *M*.

telephone talk

Ages: 9 months and up

Materials
2 play telephones

Instead of getting baby one play telephone, get two, so baby can have real conversations with you. At first you will just be babbling to each other, taking turns of course, but later baby will begin to copy how you talk on the phone. What better way to begin to learn the rules of conversation?

★ Wit & Wisdom ★
Whenever I clean the house, I give my son a big soft bristle paintbrush to sweep up the crumbs.
—Rita B., Scottsdale, Arizona

mirror magic

Ages: 6 to 12 months

Sit on the floor and hold baby on your lap looking into a floor mirror. Touch baby's head, eyes, ears, nose, and chin, naming each part as you sing the following song to the tune of "Here We Go 'Round the Mulberry Bush":

This is what I call my head
Call my head, call my head.
This is what I call my head,
Listen, look, and see.
Now I know the parts of me,
Parts of me, parts of me.
Now I know the parts of me,
Listen, look, and see.
(repeat, adding other body parts)

Make funny faces and encourage baby to imitate; wiggle your tongue side to side, stick your tongue in and out, puff your cheeks up with air, or blow a kiss. Then when baby begins to change expression, imitate baby's funny faces.

give me

Ages: 12 to 18 months

This game can be played anywhere. It teaches baby what the words "give me" mean, as well as introducing baby to the concept of sharing an object without losing it. Sit facing baby. Find an interesting toy to hand to baby and, as you do, say, "(your name) is giving baby the (object name)." Let baby look at the toy and play with it a bit as you use descriptive words to talk about the toy. Then say, "Baby give (your name) the (object name)," hold out your hand, say thank you, and smile as baby hands it to you. Repeat with other toys. As baby gets older, you can make it more fun and a bit harder by saying, "Give me a yellow toy," or "Give me a small doll," letting baby go and find what you asked for.

baby's poem

Ages: 12 months and up

As baby grows and begins to recognize words for everyday things, such as "cup," "baby," "juice," "bottle," "mama," or "daddy," and has one or two words to say, then it's time to compose a poem. Let the whole family get involved making a list of baby's own words, and other words that baby would recognize. Using the list, let each person come up with a sentence or two to create a heartwarming ditty sure to leave everyone smiling.

★ Wit & Wisdom ★

I never had time to record events in my second baby's baby book. Instead I decided to use our family calendar and write one thing on it each day. I saved the calendars and now have a more accurate and memorable account of my baby's first few years.
—Trish M., Indianapolis, Indiana

who says MOOO?

Ages: 12 months and up

Collect pictures of different animals from magazines, postcards, stickers, cards, and posters. Old calendars are a great buy in stores at year-end and have large colorful pictures of many animals baby is certain to know. Laminate the pictures. Look at the animal pictures with baby. Spread them on the floor around you and play WHO SAYS _____? (fill in blank with the animal sound). Use these laminated pictures to sing "Old Macdonald Had a Farm." Let baby point to or pick up the picture of the animal he or she wants to sing about next. Then, pointing to the picture, sing the next verse.

expressing emotion

Ages: 12 months and up

When a baby is having a tantrum, which is different than just crying, it is important to help her or him get out of the tantrum. Children do not typically enjoy feeling bad or out of control, and tantrums indicate a child who is out of control with his or her emotions. They may or may not know why they are throwing tantrums, however, as an adult we can help them! By putting words to the baby's behavior, we validate their feelings. For example, "Suzie, I see you are upset, your kicking and screaming tells me you are very (sad, mad, angry, frustrated). It is hard when you can't get what you want. Let's try a hug, maybe a hug will squeeze out the bad feelings, come here, let's see...." Even when a child is not throwing a tantrum, it is important to acknowledge and validate his or her feelings. This is important for healthy development of self-esteem, self-awareness, and confidence.

where game

Ages: 12 months and up

Hold baby and ask "where" questions like: Where is baby's bed? Where is baby's nose? Where is mommy's room? When baby is very small and doesn't know how to point, he or she may simply look in that direction. Walk where baby looks and say, "There is baby's bed!" Even if baby doesn't seem to know, answer each question yourself, going toward the object you asked about. When baby is older, he or she will point themselves, and later will run to show you.

★ **Wit & Wisdom** ★

I never seemed to get enough water when I was nursing, especially in the middle of the night since I was too tired to walk to the kitchen. I found a great solution: I fill a water bottle with ice and water before I go to bed and place it next to my baby's bed.
—Lyn H., Reno, Nevada

big or little sorting game

Ages: 18 months and up

Collect different sizes of the same types of objects for baby to arrange by size. This could be shoes, boxes, shells, stones, books, silverware, toys, blocks, bowls, or balls. In each group of objects, ask baby to choose the big _____ then the small _____. If there are more than two of an object, encourage baby to arrange them in order from biggest to smallest. Baby might decide to create an arrangement with all the objects that has nothing to do with size, but pleases baby immensely. Respect baby's hard work. You might also try sorting games where objects are arranged by color, shape, or other category features.

31

feeding fun

playing the breast-feeding game

Best Tips

- During the first month or so when your breasts are full and hard, place a heating pad on your breasts before nursing.
- When baby begins teething, give him or her a frozen teething ring, or a clean wash cloth that has been soaked and frozen before you nurse. Once baby is actively nursing, he or she can't bite because of tongue position, so make sure to quickly remove baby from your breast by gently inserting your pinkie into baby's mouth, as soon as baby is finished.
- Use your nursing time to totally relax, breath deeply, talk with baby, or close your eyes and meditate. If you have other children, begin the ritual early of having something quiet to do whenever you nurse.
- Get support from other nursing mothers or organizations when frustrated.

Maintaining Your Milk Supply

- If your milk supply is low, nurse or pump more frequently until your flow resumes. Try to empty each breast twice as often as you normally would each day.
- Cuddle while you nurse. Skin-to-skin contact triggers hormones that stimulate milk production.
- Nurse before offering baby cereal or other foods.
- A natural way to increase supply is fenugreek, a seed that is available in capsule form at most health-food stores.

high chair shenanigans

Ages: 9 months and up

Spoons and Language
Using two different spoons, one for baby and one for caregiver, introduce the concepts of same and different, mine and yours, as well as concepts like put in, take out, open (mouth), and close. The best way for baby to learn words and concepts is through active participation.

Chair Entertainment
Some ideas in case baby gets bored before you finish your dinner:

- Give baby a plastic bath book to look at.
- Mix up some instant pudding to spread on the tray like finger paint.
- Mix fruit with yogurt and freeze it in ice-cube trays; tastes great, great for teething, and best of all, baby will be challenged and occupied getting it into her mouth!

apricot and apple puree

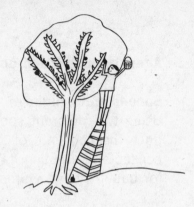

Ages: 4 months and up

Ingredients
½ cup dried apricots
2 sweet apples (use less of these ingredients
if you do not want to freeze leftovers)

Directions
Rinse the dried apricots, then cover with cold water and soak overnight.
Simmer gently in the same water for about 25 minutes, or until very soft
and pulpy. Cool. In the meantime, peel and core apples. Cook the sliced
apple in a little water or apple juice until it is soft. Puree the apricots
and apples. Freeze leftovers in ice-cube trays.

Note: If possible, buy dried fruit that has been naturally dried and is
unsulfured. If the fruit has been sulfur-dried, it needs to be washed in
hot water before use.

vegetable custard

Ages: 6 months and up

Ingredients
¼ cup pureed vegetables
(sweet potato, pumpkin, carrots, or squash)
1 egg yolk, beaten
¼ cup milk or formula

Directions
Preheat oven to 375°F (190°C). Blend together ingredients and pour into a buttered ovenproof dish or individual custard cups. Place dish in a pan with 1 inch water in it and bake for 30 minutes. (Wherever milk is called for, soybean milk could also be used.)

★ Wit & Wisdom ★

The best thing I ever did in the kitchen was to clear out one whole drawer for my baby. I put plastic cups, pans, bowls, spoons, and all sorts of safe gadgets in it. My baby learned that it was the only drawer or cabinet in the kitchen to play in. I would change the contents regularly to keep it interesting.
—Julia Y., Walnut Creek, California

yogurt plus

Ages: 8 months and up

- **Banana Yogurt:** Mix a mashed banana with homemade yogurt.
- **Apple Yogurt:** 3 tablespoons plain yogurt, 2 tablespoons applesauce. Place ingredients in a blender and puree. Any fruit puree may be used.
- **Carob Yogurt:** 2 tablespoons plain yogurt, 1 teaspoon carob powder (8 months). Sprinkle carob over yogurt, mix, and serve.
- **Yogurt Ice:** Mix yogurt with any fruit puree in season and pour into ice-cube trays. Partially freeze, then add sticks, and freeze until firm. Keep a close eye on the sticks and take them away as soon as baby finishes.
- **Wheat Germ Breakfast:** (Don't give wheat germ to babies under 6 months) 1 tablespoon wheat germ, 2 tablespoons plain yogurt, 1 teaspoon maple syrup, 1 tablespoon pureed raw apple or mashed banana. Mix all ingredients together and serve.

★ Wit & Wisdom ★

I keep a basket filed with things I often need while I breast-feed my daughter; a cloth for burping, the TV remote, a portable phone, mail, books, or a magazine. When my daughter gets hungry, I grab the basket and I'm ready.
—Gladis G., Boston, Massachusetts

mashed potato sculpture

Ages: 12 months and up

Prepare instant mashed potatoes however you like them. Put a stiff pile of potatoes on baby's tray and give her a variety of foods to stick into the potatoes, creating a food sculpture. She may also like modeling the potatoes like play dough into shapes, or using spoons, cups, or other kitchen supplies.

guess the scent

Ages: 15 months and up

Put together containers of foods that have various smells: cinnamon, pepper, lemon, vanilla, chocolate, popcorn, tuna, cheese, etc. Make a game out of guessing the smells. Have baby put hands over eyes and smell. Even if baby can't name the smell, he or she will have fun learning what the word smell means. Play this game often whenever you are cooking and baby is near.

★ **Wit & Wisdom** ★

Whenever I bake bread, pizza dough, or pretzels with my 15-month-old, I spray her hands with cooking spray. It isn't as messy as oil or butter and it keeps her hands from sticking to the dough.
—Jill B., Grafton, Wisconsin

chocolate-dipped fruit

Ages: 12 months and up

Ingredients
Bananas, strawberries, cantaloupe
½ pound semisweet white or dark chocolate
1 tablespoon solid vegetable shortening
Toothpicks or skewers

Directions
Wash strawberries and pat dry with a paper towel. Peel bananas and cut cantaloupe into large chunks. In a double boiler over hot but not boiling water, melt chocolate and vegetable shortening, stirring carefully. Leave the bottom of the double boiler on the flame and take the top with the chocolate in it to your work surface and pour chocolate into a small bowl so baby can help you dip. If the chocolate begins to harden, return it to the heat. Stick a toothpick or skewer into each piece of fruit. Dip ⅔ of the fruit into the chocolate coating, letting the excess chocolate drip back into the pan. Chill fruit until chocolate is hardened.

Note: A good way to let the chocolate harden is to stick the toothpicks into a Styrofoam block covered with plastic wrap.

designer pancakes

Ages: 12 months and up

Ingredients
1½ cups low-fat milk
4 tablespoons vegetable oil
2 eggs
2 teaspoons baking powder
1½ cups flour
Oil or butter for frying

Directions
Put ingredients in a bowl and mix. Heat skillet over medium heat and add 2 tablespoons of oil. When a drop of water dances on the surface of the skillet, you are ready to begin your art! Using a large spoon, make a design by dribbling the pancake mix into the skillet. Children are very good at making drip designs; just be sure their arms are clear of the skillet sides. Make sure that designs are small enough to fit inside a pancake. Cook design for 30 seconds. Pour ¼ cup of the remaining batter on top of the design and wait until pancake has bubbles on it before turning it over (1 to 2 minutes). Turn pancake and brown the other side. Cover with syrup or jam and eat!

Note: Pour pancake or cupcake batter into a quart milk container for easy pouring.

from bottle to straw

Ages: 15 months and up

The sippy cup, although convenient, is not the best for oral development. The tongue position that occurs while sipping from a sippy cup imitates the position during nursing or bottle-feeding. A straw or open cup requires a more mature oral posture from the child and is better for language development. Use a thicker liquid when introducing a straw or open cup so baby will not spill as easily or choke on too much liquid. Try applesauce or yogurt with a bit of juice or water. Initially, cut the straw so baby can pull the drink up without getting too frustrated.

★ Wit & Wisdom ★

It was easy to wean my daughter from her bottle. I cut the tip off the bottle nipple, inverted it, and then inserted a straw through the hole. My daughter enjoyed the familiar feel of her bottle and quickly learned to use a straw.
—Janet E., Indiana, Pennsylvania

41

playing the on-the-go food game

- To avoid having to pack snacks every time you leave the house, keep a plastic box filled with snacks under the seat of your car. Include juice boxes, water, hand wipes, and nonperishable finger foods, as well as a trash bag.
- For long car rides, pack snacks and place them in a paper bag. At designated times, let baby pick a snack. Make sure to stop the car, get out, and let baby stretch during snack time.
- On vacation, try to stick to baby's established eating schedule.
- If you need a bottle warmed up, ask the waiter or waitress to bring a glass half filled with hot water. Place the bottle in the glass and in a few minutes it will be ready.
- When eating in a restaurant, ask for dip for baby's food: syrup for waffles, ranch dressing for veggies, and ketchup for fries and fish sticks. Kids enjoy dipping each bite, which gives you time to eat your own meal.
- Pick restaurants that cater to families; they have high chairs, serve food quickly, expect a little noise, and have cheerful servers who like waiting on families.

water and
bath activities

newborn bathtime

Ages: o to 6 months

- Make sure the bathroom temperature is warm.
- Many small tubs are available at baby stores. Put only a few inches of water in to begin with. Smile at baby and encourage him or her to kick and play. Gradually begin scooping up water to pour over baby's body. The goal is to help baby fully enjoy the sensation of the water.
- Play soothing music while baby is being bathed. Sing to baby during bathtime to make the first experience with water peaceful. If you are a new parent and nervous about the first few bathtimes, ask a grandparent, friend, or experienced someone to be there—just having someone by your side will give you more confidence.
- If two adults are available, one can get into the bath with baby holding baby close or letting baby lie on top of the adult's stomach as the water inches up. The second adult needs to be ready to take baby and wrap him or her in a towel when bathtime is over, so the bathing adult can get out of the tub. Trying to climb out of a bath with a slippery baby is dangerous.

simple bath toys

Ages: 6 months and up

Developmental toys like shape sorters and stacking rings aren't limited to the living-room floor. In fact, babies who won't sit long enough to play educational games out of water just might enjoy them at bathtime.

Homemade fun: Use cookie cutters or stencils to trace shapes on a colorful rubber place mat. Then cut out the shapes and let baby stick them to the sides of the tub and tiles.

Any kind of plastic bottle that squirts is great fun—prepare to be squirted!

Soap crayons and bath paints are a must since the bathtub is the ultimate location for messy art experimentation.

★ Wit & Wisdom ★

My daughter loved it whenever I did silly things. One of her favorite bath games was bubble disguise. I'd use the bubbles from the bathtub to make up various disguises; beards, long or short hair, or a big round nose. In the beginning, she would just look at me and laugh, but as she got older, she wanted to make up disguises too.
—Beth W., Brooklyn, New York

bubble fun

Mild recipe
⅓ cup tearless baby shampoo
1¼ cup water
2 teaspoons sugar
1 drop food coloring

Strong, thick recipe
¼ cup clear liquid dishwashing detergent
¼ cup glycerin (from drugstore)
¾ cup water
1 tablespoon sugar

Combine the ingredients and pour the bubble solution into an unbreakable container with a lid. Babies are fascinated with bubbles. Many toy stores offer a variety of bubble-blowing options to create bubbles of different sizes and shapes. Baby will try to catch bubbles as they drift toward the water, or watch them magically fall all around him or her. Huge bubbles are especially fun when baby can be the first to pop them. Let older babies blow their own bubbles.

toys play hide and seek

Ages: 9 months and up

This game of hide and seek features plastic lids turned upside down hiding a toy underneath. To play, toss six or more plastic lids onto the surface of the water, where they should all float. Ask baby to close his or her eyes while you hide a small plastic floating toy under one of the lids. Baby then guesses where the toy is, lifting lid after lid until he or she discovers it. Then it is baby's turn to hide the toy while you shut your eyes.

★ **Wit & Wisdom** ★

My baby hated having her hair washed until I let her help me. We filled an empty ketchup bottle with water. Her job was to get her hair wet by squirting the water on her head. I also bought her a pair of junior swim goggles so that the soap didn't get in her eyes.
—Jessica S., North Andover, Massachusetts

string of floaters

47

Materials
Styrofoam (from grocery trays, box packing, etc.)
Corks
Sponges
Small, thin wood pieces
Lightweight string

Cut the Styrofoam or sponge into shapes. Poke holes in the Styrofoam, sponges, wood, and corks. Thread the string through the hole in each of the objects. Tie the ends of the string together so that the objects are hanging like a necklace. Put the string of floaters in the bath, lake, river, or in an outside wading pool.

★ **Wit & Wisdom** ★
Put food coloring in water, then pour into ice-cube trays. Dump frozen ice cubes into bath. Baby will have so much fun trying to pick them up!
—Toni T., Salinas, California

tea for two

Ages: 15 months and up

Pouring is a favorite activity, and what better place to practice than in the tub where a spill doesn't matter. Put a clean plastic stepstool in the center of the bath, making sure the water doesn't come more than halfway up the stool legs, or the stool will begin to float. Help baby set the table with plastic dishes, a tea set, cups, plates, and cutlery for two. Use washcloths for tablecloth and napkins. If you don't have plastic play food to serve as snacks, cut shapes out of clean kitchen sponges.

48

★ Wit & Wisdom ★

I couldn' t figure out why my son, Jared, was always soaking his diapers. One day a girl-friend was over and told me I should point his penis downward when diapering to pre-vent leaks—since then, no soaked diapers.
—Sharon P., Charlotte, North Carolina

freeze dance

Ages: 12 months and up

This is a great game to play with baby, siblings, or friends. Someone stands by the sprinkler to turn it on and off. Encourage baby to dance around under the sprinkler. When the water turns off, everyone has to freeze. It might take baby a while to catch on—most likely she will simply stop dancing and laugh when everyone else stops.

★ Wit & Wisdom ★

My son loved watching the rainbow we'd create with a garden hose. He especially liked doing this once he learned the words "light" and "dark." We'd watch the rainbow come and go as we moved the water stream around.
—Jennifer F., Glen Ellyn, Illinois

49

frozen treasures

Materials
Clean paper milk carton, quart and half-gallon sizes
Small plastic toys safe for baby; figures of zoo animals and sea life work well

Fill the milk carton with water and several small figures. Place it in the freezer until frozen solid. When it is frozen, remove the ice block from the carton and place it in a plastic tub for baby to explore. Touch the ice with baby and talk about what you are feeling. Slide objects on the surface. For baby's bath, place the block into the bathtub. Watch what happens as the ice slowly melts. Is the bath water surrounding the block cooler? Can baby see what's inside the block? During summer months, ice blocks large and small are fun to play with outside. Baby learns how water changes shape and can magically evaporate.

water painting

Ages: 15 months and up

Materials
Old paintbrushes
Bucket or cup of water
Construction paper or brown paper bags

With an ordinary paintbrush and a bucket or cup of water, baby can decorate rocks, paint disappearing scenes on pavement, and even paint construction or brown paper bags and watch water magically disappear. Try making hand prints on the bag or point out how a rock changes from gray to black. Baby will love making a shape, then seeing it disappear as the sun dries the pavement. There is no mess to clean up, water is free, and baby will be happily entertained!

★ **Wit & Wisdom** ★

Whenever I'm playing outside with my kids, I put our garbage can at the end of the driveway. Of course, I still have to keep a close eye on my kids so they won't go into the street, but the garbage can keeps cars from entering the driveway or using it to turn around.
—Amy E., Apple Valley, California

some float, some don't

Ages: 18 months and up

Materials
Clear plastic container or tub
Variety of household items: sponge, clothespin, spoon,
key, plastic toy, cup, wood block, comb, shell, paper, etc.
Beach towel

Spread towel out on the floor over a low table, or outside if the weather is warm. Fill the container two-thirds full with water and place it on the towel. Set the items you have chosen on the towel next to the container. Baby will probably begin putting the items into the water without much prompting from you. Say, "Let's see which things stay on top of the water and which things fall to the bottom." Use the words "float" and "sink" as you notice where each item is, and talk about what they're made of: wood, metal, plastic, sponge, etc. Remember, the questions you ask out loud are to encourage baby to think scientifically and develop observation skills; don't worry whether the answer is right or wrong. Encourage observation of life!

happy helper

Ages: 15 months and up

Baby loves to help around the house, and jobs that involve water are a big hit.

Window washing: Pour two tablespoons of white vinegar into a small spray bottle and fill it with water. Show baby how to spray the window, then polish it with a paper towel.

Floor mopping: Put about four inches of warm soapy water into a cleaning bucket (one or two drops of mild liquid dish soap will do). Put two sponges in the bucket, and work together on a small area. Show baby how to squeeze the extra water out of the sponge before putting it on the floor.

Dishwashing: Put dishwashing soap in the sink to create lots of bubbles. Put a stool up next to the sink and let baby have fun washing plastic play dishes. Baby can use the dish brush that you use and set the clean dishes on a towel. Baby can even dry the dishes and put them away in the play kitchen or toy box. This will give baby something to do while you are cooking dinner!

★ Wit & Wisdom ★

Punch holes in the bottom of a plastic container and fill it with water to enjoy the shower effect.
—Mary W., Atlanta, Georgia

53

bubbles and waves

Ages: 18 months and up

Materials
Kitchen egg beater
Wire whisks, spoons, etc.
Straws or plastic tubing
Floating boat or block

Put together a bucket of fun for bathtub play. Place the boat or toy in the water. Use the egg beater to create waves behind the boat, making the boat move through the water. The straw or tubing can be used to blow bubbles. Get a second piece of tubing long enough so you can enjoy blowing bubbles from outside the bath. The spoons and whisk can be used for splashing. The idea is to make bathtime fun and make water a friend.

★ Wit & Wisdom ★

Put a bath towel down on the bottom of the tub; that way babies can lie on their back and kick as much as they want without sliding. Of course, make sure there are only a few inches of water in the bath.
—Todd P., St. Cloud, Minnesota

playing the sunscreen game

Sun protection is very important for preventing skin damage. Even gloomy, cold, winter days can present sun hazards if baby is outside for more than fifteen minutes.

- For babies over six months old, apply sunscreen thirty minutes before going outside to all parts of the body that will be exposed to the sun. Make sure the sunscreen if at least 15 SPF and that the package says it blocks A and B ultraviolet rays.
- Don't use sunscreen on babies younger than six months. That means you have to protect your baby by dressing accordingly. Buy several cute sun hats with wide brims, a robe, long sleeved lightweight clothing, and an umbrella for the beach.
- Play a "dress up for the sun game" to get baby involved in learning about the sun. Have a supply of adult-size sun hats, as well as long-sleeved shirts and other clothing on hand. Draw a picture of the sun and hold it overhead, making up silly words while you put on the sun clothes.

★ **Wit & Wisdom** ★

I find my kids like to copy me—if I wear a hat and put sunscreen on then they want it too. We also make a game out of dressing up to meet the sun with our special clothes.
—Chris, Olcott, New York

playing the water safety game

Water is both fun and dangerous for baby. She can drown in as little as two inches of water—the amount that can cover her mouth and nose—if not closely watched. Hazards can be as obvious as the ocean, a swimming pool, or any other large body of water; or, they can be as commonplace as a bathtub, a public fountain, a wading pool, or a back-yard birdbath. Babies must be watched anytime they are around water!

- Never leave baby alone in the bath. Always make sure that you have soap, towels, shampoo, and bath toys ready before putting baby in the tub. Once she is in the tub, ignore phone calls and doorbells.
- Teach your baby to swim so that baby learns to enjoy water, but never be lulled into believing that your baby is water safe.
- Before taking kids anywhere near water, make sure one supervising adult knows how to swim. Learn CPR.
- If you have children of different ages, bring a blow-up pool to place away from the lake or ocean so that older kids who are ready to play in the ocean or lake have the opportunity to play, while infants have their own water fun in the baby pool.
- Establish clear rules to be followed regarding water play. No turning bath water on without a parent in attendance, no getting into the baby pool or bathtub without parent, etc. Teach kids to appreciate that water is fun, but can also be dangerous.

bedtime

playing the sleep game

- Establish a regular bedtime for your baby and try to stick to it. Look for signs you baby is winding down and ready to nod off, for many baby's as early as 7 or 8 p.m. If you miss that opportunity, you have an overly tired child who will grow agitated.
- Set up a bedtime ritual. Routine is important for a child's sense of security. Make the routine brief—no more than 30 minutes—so it's clear that bedtime is coming. You might feed her, then read a story or sing a song, change her then rock or massage her. Familiar sights, smells, and sounds also help to signal sleep, so play the same bedtime tape or music box, or put something in baby's room that smells like you. You might also have a special stuffed toy that never leaves the crib so baby associates it with sleep.
- Teach baby to nod off by himself. By six weeks, try not to let baby fall asleep while you're feeding or rocking him. Otherwise he might not learn how to fall asleep unless you're there to help him. The trick is to put him in his crib while he's drowsy but still awake.
- Once baby knows how to drift off to sleep on her own, you can wake her up for a feeding before you are ready to go to bed which might prevent baby waking up just as you're nodding off.
- When you do feed baby during the night, keep the lights dim, talk little, be as boring as possible. What you don't want to become is baby's 4 a.m. playmate.

when baby won't play the sleep game

There are many books written on this subject and they support many different theories. Here are a few points that may help.

- Babies rarely sleep through the night before three months, and then, through the night usually means from midnight to 6 a.m.
- Start observing what baby is waking up for. Is baby hungry or does he just want to see you?
- If baby is six months to a year old and still not sleeping through the night, you may want to try sleep training them. Some parents fear their baby might feel abandoned if they are left to cry, but most child-development specialists believe that letting a baby cry so he can learn to fall asleep on his own is healthier in the long run.

Steps to take:

1. Decide on a strategy with your spouse. How long will you let the baby cry, who will go in to reassure him?
2. Start off slowly: follow the usual bedtime routine; if she protests when you put her in her crib let her cry for the decided amount of time. After the allotted time is up go and calm her without picking her up, then leave the room again. Each time stay away for a little longer.
3. You don't have to follow this pattern whenever your baby wakes up during the night for it to succeed. Simply doing it each night at bedtime can establish the correct pattern.

rock-a-baby game

Ages: o and up

Baby will love your voice no matter how it sounds, so don't eliminate singing based on your own self-critical view of your voice. Sing lullabies to baby that will soothe both of you. If you don't know any, buy a lullaby tape and memorize a few. Rock together, holding baby close as you sing softly. Here is one to try:

Sleep, baby, sleep
Sleep, baby, sleep, thy father guards the sheep.
Thy mother shakes the dreamland tree, and from it fall
sweet dreams for thee.
Sleep, baby, sleep.

Smile, baby, smile, thy mother guards awhile.
Thy father tends the dreamland tree,
and shakes a new sweet dream for thee.
Smile, baby, smile.

Reprinted with permission from "Father Gander Nursery Rhymes," by Dr. Douglas W. Larche, published by Advocacy Press.

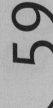

together time

Ages: 0 and up

Pick one hour each night, about the time baby goes to bed, and make a rule. No phone calls or visitors during that hour. That way you can peacefully put baby to bed without being interrupted or distracted. Once baby is in bed, you will hopefully be left with some time together, or to relax on your own. Once the hour is up, you can go on with life as usual. This action is a constant reminder that family matters.

69

★ **Wit & Wisdom** ★

Every night, about an hour before my kids are supposed to go to bed, I start whispering. It seems to calm the whole house down.
—Ashley T., La Honda, California

bedtime tape

Ages: 3 months and up

Materials
Tape recorder
Blank cassette tape
Child's favorite storybook

Make a cassette tape to play each night as baby goes to sleep. Record songs, poems, stories, or anything else baby likes. The important thing is for baby to hear your familiar voice. This is also perfect for the times baby goes to Grandma and Grandpa's, to a baby-sitter, or when you are out of town.

★ **Wit & Wisdom** ★

Before I go to bed each night, I put a few quiet time activities in a special basket for my two-year-old to do when she wakes up in the morning. I usually get a little extra sleep!
—George W., Milwaukee, WI

61

kiss me game

Ages: 3 months and up

This game teaches body parts at the same time as you touch and bond with each other. Start with a nose kiss, that is, rubbing your noses together, move to your chins and rub them together, your foreheads, ears, eyes, eyelashes, hair and so on. Don't forget feet, elbows, knees and stomach. Baby will giggle with delight and will ask to carry out this tradition each night, and still be asking you for various "kisses" when they are five! This is great for bonding as well as body part identification as baby gets older.

★ Wit & Wisdom ★

The best thing I ever put in my son's room was a spare twin mattress placed on the floor. When he was a baby it made a great reading corner, and as he grew, it had many uses: for tumbling, wrestling, bouncing, fort construction, not to mention it gave me a place to sleep when he was sick.
—Brian T., St. Cloud, Minnesota

peace hug

Ages: 6 months and up

A peace hug is when you hold baby long enough so that *you* relax completely, letting all your tensions dissolve as you breathe. When you are very tense it may take five minutes to relax, so hold on until you feel peace wash over you. Feel baby breathing and breathe with him. This hug works wonders if you have just lost your temper over something your child has done. Better yet, instead of losing your temper in the first place, try a peace hug.

★ **Wit & Wisdom** ★

"We cannot start too early in giving a child continuous, warm, consistent affection. He simply must have this unconditional love to cope most effectively in today's world."
—Dr. Ross Campbell

flashlight games

Ages: 9 months and up

These games might be a fun addition to your bedtime ritual.

Flashing colors. Turn off the lights. Put a colored scarf or tissue over the end of the flashlight and project colors onto the wall.

I spot. Turn the light off and shine the flashlight on different spots around baby's room, on her toys, pictures, or clock.

Light chaser. You direct the light along a path and have baby crawl to catch the light.

★ Wit & Wisdom ★

When you look in on your baby at night, are you afraid you'll wake her if you turn on the light? I was, so I decided to try a red light bulb in the light on her dresser. It casts a calming glow, without being bright.
—Amanda H., Eugene, Oregon

dream pillow

Ages: 9 months and up

Materials
White pillowcase
Fabric paint (non-toxic)
Piece of cardboard

Make a good-dream pillow. Before you start painting, put the piece of cardboard in between the pillowcase. Draw an angel, a teddy bear, a picture of mom, dad, brothers, and sisters, handprints of members of the family with the words, "my hands are always holding you," or whatever you think baby would recognize and like on the pillowcase. You might also have a photo of baby silk-screened onto the pillowcase. This pillowcase can travel wherever baby goes. It's an easy way to bring baby's secure feelings to wherever he sleeps. Make sure to wash it before using to soften the paint.

★ Wit & Wisdom ★
My daughter loves to take off her clothes, so to keep her from taking off her one-piece pajamas, I cut off the feet and turned them backwards. Now she can't reach the zipper.
—Clara W., San Jose, California

imagine

Ages: 6 months and up

When children are falling asleep, a peaceful state is at hand. This is the time to tell them an "Imagine" story. It is different from a regular story. You are going to merely suggest what direction the child's mind goes, letting them wander around in their own thoughts a bit. This could be called a guided meditation. When a baby is small, you could start telling stories each night about a special place he might be familiar with, like a garden, meadow, or grove of trees. Describe this place slowly in a soft voice and in great detail. Tell him to try to see this place in his mind. Talk about the friendly animals, a wise person or guardian angel, and a large rock where he can leave his worries. Make up all sorts of stories using this setting. When baby is old enough to follow the story, you will lead him into his special place through your words, then leave him on his own in silence for a few minutes to interact and imagine. As you lead him out of his place, talk about how his good feelings will go with him, and that whenever he wants to visit this place, he can in his own mind. Be creative and try to incorporate any problem areas you see. For example, if he is afraid of people, bring some people into the scene and talk about all the fun they are having together.

teeth brushing

Ages: 12 months and up

When babies are just getting teeth, give them a toothbrush to chew on. As they begin to brush their teeth with your help, here are a few ideas to make them like it more.

- Talk to their teeth, make up a running story as you brush. Have baby open his mouth wide so you can see the characters you are talking about.
- Let baby brush your teeth after you have brushed his.
- Give her a small flashlight and let her look at your teeth. This might generate interest in the subject.
- Take photos and make up a story about (baby's) tooth brushing magic. Read baby the story before brushing teeth.
- Most drug stores sell finger cots or a rubber toothbrush for babies, they fit on an adult's finger and enable you to rub gums and new teeth with soft rubber bristles. You can also use a wet washcloth to gently massage teething gums.

★ Wit & Wisdom ★

I could never get my baby to sit still while I brushed her teeth until one day my six-year-old suggested that we turn off the lights and shine a flashlight on Megan's teeth while I brushed.
—Patty White, Greer, South Carolina

baby's room

safety tips

- Keep baby's bed free of long ribbons, cords, or hanging toys that baby might reach.
- Keep lamp and appliance cords out of reach so that baby can't tug or chew on them.
- As soon as baby can crawl, cover unused electrical outlets with safety caps.
- Screen off unguarded heaters.
- Keep crib and playpen away from windows so baby can't pull down curtains or crawl out the window.
- Don't put any climbable objects near windows and don't put toys in crib that baby could stack in order to climb out.
- Store toys and games low, and dangerous objects high out of reach, or locked up.
- Position hanging hooks above child's eye level.
- Remove small objects baby could choke on.
- Check any paint suspected of being used before 1978 for lead poisoning.
- Install smoke detectors, and if baby's room is on the second floor purchase one of the rope ladders now available through children's catalogs.
- For baby products that have warnings or recalls call the Consumer Product Safety Commission at (800) 638-2772.

stuffed animal solutions

Ages: 0 months and up

Animal Hammock: Find an unused corner of the bedroom and make a hammock where the stuffed animals can rest. Cut a piece of fabric to fit the shape of the corner then add 4 inches. Sew the edges under, then nail or thumb tack to the wall. If you have lots of animals, try hammock bunk beds.

Bear Wreath: Go to a craft store and buy a large wreath form. Attach each stuffed animal with floral wire. Hang on baby's wall.

Critter Pole: Measure baby's room from floor to ceiling. Buy a 2- to 3-inch-diameter dowel from a building supply store. Have the store cut the dowel according to your floor to ceiling measurement. Buy a set of flat wooden brackets that the dowel can slide into to hold it in place on the ceiling and floor. Purchase a packet of small screw-in hooks. Paint the pole to match baby's room. When dry, screw in the hooks to accommodate as many stuffed animals as you'd like to hang. Slide the dowel into the floor and ceiling brackets. Hang stuffed animals.

baby's dresser and storage tips

Ages: 0 months and up

Buy a dresser at a garage sale. Paint it a bright color. Then search for old toy cars or other small toys that would work as drawer pulls. Drill holes in the toys, add spacers to make sure they stand away from the drawers and then screw them into the drawers.

Instead of buying a dresser, buy inexpensive canvas sweater organizers and hang them in the closet. Your baby will gain floor space in her bedroom for play time and all her clothes will be visible, organized and out of reach.

Take a look at the baby-wipe boxes next time you're shopping. Pick a brand that has a colorful sturdy design so that you can recycle the boxes as storage containers for all the small toys, puzzles, and pieces to come. Place a sticker or a picture of the toy pieces being stored in the box so it can be easily identified. Since they stack easily, everything stays neat, tidy, and organized.

allergy-free

Ages: 0 months and up

If allergies run in your family, here are a few things you can do to minimize suffering in the baby's room:

1. Encase mattress in a dustproof, plastic, zip-shut mattress bag. Call an allergist's office and ask them for a recommended company to buy the bag from.
2. Avoid upholstered furniture.
3. Choose synthetic materials rather than natural fibers, a polyester-filled pillow rather than feathers, nylon carpet instead of wool, etc. Sheets and blankets can be cotton if washed frequently (the house dust mite is a common allergen and it lives off natural fibers).
4. Have only washable stuffed animals and wash them once a month.
5. Have hardwood floors if possible, using throw rugs on top that can be washed.
6. Keep surfaces clear so they can be dusted or vacuumed two to three times per week.
7. Keep all pets with fur, hair, or feathers out of baby's room.

wall mural

Ages: o months and up

Materials
Overhead projector (borrow one from
  school or local library)
Plastic overhead sheet
Black overhead marker
Picture of mural to be painted on wall
Acrylic paint tubes (bought at art supply stores)
Paintbrushes

Look through picture books or at greeting cards for ideas of pictures, characters, or scenery to paint as a mural on the wall. Decide which wall to put the mural on. Put the plastic sheet over the picture you wish to paint on the wall and trace it with the black marker. Turn on the overhead projector and place the plastic sheet on top. Move the overhead projector around until the image is shining on the wall in the position you want. You may have to move the machine forward or backward to get the image size you want. Using a pencil, trace the overhead projected lines onto the wall. Turn off the projector and paint in the colors with acrylic paint. Use a black paint pen to do the outline after all the colored acrylic paint has dried.

penny wish container

Ages: 0 months and up

Materials
Pretty glass container
Lots of pennies
Decorative notebook or journal

Whenever a friend or family member comes to visit, ask them to make a penny wish for baby, and put it in the special container in baby's room far out of baby's reach. Place a small notebook next to the container so friends and family can write and date their wish. Begin this tradition when baby is born and keep it up as baby grows.

One day, you will be able to celebrate with him, as you share how many people have wished good things for his life. The tradition could continue throughout life, maybe once a year on his birthday. No matter where he lives or how old he is, you can send him a penny wish in an envelope!

baby's own time capsule

Ages: 0 months and up

Create a special box of some sort to keep all baby's treasures until it's time for her to leave home. It could be a wooden box, or a cardboard box. Whatever you choose, make it special. Put baby's first pair of shoes in it, clothing worn home from the hospital, first hair cut, a cassette tape with first noises and words, hand and feet prints, special cards written to baby, a small picture album, and first drawing. You get the idea, so make it a big box! It has to hold all of baby's treasures throughout her life.

★ Wit & Wisdom ★

When my daughter was a newborn, I didn't "sleep when the baby sleeps," as everyone advises new parents, and I still don't. But instead of cleaning and paying bills during that precious time like I used to, I now read a book for at least a half-hour every nap. The escape is incredible and completely rejuvenating. My working-mom friend does the same during her lunch breaks. Best of all, now she and I can talk about books instead of potty training when we're together.
—Amber, Denver, Colorado

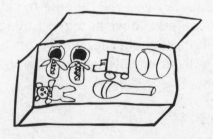

what's hanging?

Materials
Ceiling hook used for hanging plants
Yarn or string
Things to hang: scarves, party or holiday decorations, small figures, or stuffed animals

Attach the ceiling hook into the ceiling directly above baby's bed. Tie the string securely to whatever object is being hung. Lower the object seven to nine inches from baby's face. The lighter objects, like scarves and ribbons, will move as a breeze as a fan hits them, and will interest baby for a longer period of time than objects that hang still.

Change your objects daily. Leave the string attached and store them in a box. After a few days use the same object again. Newborn to about six-week old babies will just look at the objects. When baby begins to reach up and grab at the objects, raise the objects out of baby's reach. Don't hang anything that could hurt baby if it was pulled down.

baby's view

Ages: 3 months and up

Every day baby is placed in the same crib with his head the same direction. The car seat is on the same side of the car, and usually the high chair sits in the same location somewhere near the family table. Baby turns his head and sees the same things from these locations, which allows him to remember and record details about his environment. To give baby a new, bigger view of his environment and to challenge him to increase his memory, move things around. Rearrange baby's furniture once in a while. Place baby in the crib with his head in the opposite direction. Move the high chair so baby can look out the window instead of at a wall. Take a few minutes to think about baby's daily view, then do one thing to create a more exciting, stimulating experience.

display shelf

Ages: 9 months and up

Clear a shelf somewhere in baby's room to become baby's special museum. On this shelf you might want to start out by putting some of baby's first pictures; then, as baby gets older, display things baby finds outside, or things baby makes, or things baby has a special interest in. This shelf can include anything that is a record of baby's life or interests. When baby sees the importance of things collected or created, the feeling of being special and important will grow within him.

★ Wit & Wisdom ★

I needed a rug for the nursery so I purchased a piece of remnant carpet about ten feet by ten feet. I then found some large number and letter stencils and spray-painted them onto the rug. We have made up numerous games, and my son loves to run and touch whatever number or letter I call out.
—Elaine B., Bellevue, Washington

blackboard

Ages: 12 months and up

Materials
Blackboard paint
Any surface that is hard and smooth
(closet door, bed headboard, wall, particle board)
Paintbrush
Fine sandpaper
Paint cleaner to wash brush

If the hard surface already has some sort of paint on it, you will need to sand the surface until it feels a bit rough, as this helps the blackboard paint to "stick" better. Apply two to three coats of blackboard paint following paint instructions on the can. Once the paint has dried thoroughly, your little artist may begin. Keep a plastic container of colored chalk nearby. An old damp rag works best as an eraser because it easily removes chalk without hard rubbing.

photo wallpaper

Ages: 12 months and up

Materials
Photos of baby and family
Piece of yarn and nail
Wallpaper paste and brush
Clear gel acrylic
Clean rag

This designer wallpaper is made out of photocopied pictures glued to the wall. The results are wonderful! Choose ten black-and-white photos you like and have the negatives made into 5 x 7 or 8 x 10 black-and-white prints. Take the prints to a copy store and copy the photos onto sheets of paper. Measure the size of the wall you plan to cover with the pictures to decide how many copies of each picture will be needed. Decide on a pattern to follow. Tie a nail to a piece of yarn. Tape the yarn to the upper edge of the wall so the yarn will hang in a straight line. Once the yarn is hanging straight, tape it to the bottom of the wall. Follow this line when putting up the first row of pictures. Put wallpaper paste on the wall, then put one paper picture up at a time, rubbing over the top with a clean rag to make sure there are no bubbles. Continue in this way until all pictures are on the wall. Once the wall is dry, paint at least two coats of a gel acrylic over the top of the paper.

photo fun

Buy a frame to hold a school size photo for each child in the family.

Put a current photo of each child in individual frames. Each year put a new and current photo over the top of the old one. Keep putting the new photos over the old, letting the frame serve as storage for past years' treasures.

Buy a flat edged wooden frame. Pick out your favorite pictures of baby. Take them to a copy store and make colored copies. Using Mod Podge glue, a paint brush and a scissors, create a collage of baby on the side of the frame. If you want, add pictures from magazines or colored paper to decorate in between the pictures. Paint one or two coats of Mod Podge over finished collage. Let dry before putting your favorite picture in the frame.

rotating art display

Ages: 12 months and up

Materials
Plastic poster frames
Homemade art work

Find a place on baby's walls to hang the plastic frames. In the beginning, put paintings or drawings from siblings in the frames. When baby produces the first work of art, place it in the frame. Change the pictures within the frames weekly to display all incoming masterpieces. Keep this up as baby grows. Depending what the frame is like you may be able to store the artwork on top of each other within the frame. Another way to keep a record of baby's artwork is to take pictures of baby surrounded by a few masterpieces before you throw them away or store them. You'll have the picture to remember long after the artwork has crumpled.

★ Wit & Wisdom ★
Use snap on plastic shower curtain hooks to
attach toys to crib, stroller, or car seat.
—Allen M., Wichita, Kansas

friends and family

Materials
United States or world map
Pictures of family and friends
Lightweight paper or foam frames
Stick pins or double-sided tape

Put the map up on baby's wall. Glue the pictures into the frames and hang them on the map according to where friends and family live. Point to the pictures regularly, telling baby about people and places. It is also fun to make some sort of mark on the map on the places baby visits, along with the date of travel.

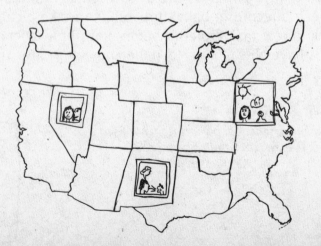

floortime

mirror magic

Ages: 3 months and up

Materials
Nonbreakable mirror
Scarf

Gaze into the mirror with baby to make faces together. Begin with no expression, and slowly change to a smiling one. Use short, descriptive phrases such as, "I look happy," "I feel silly," "See my mouth." Now, slowly change to a sad expression and say, "I look sad." Drape the scarf over the mirror and play peek-a-boo with your reflections. Say, "I see (baby's name)." Baby will gradually discover whose reflections are in the mirror, and the "magic" that makes them move. As baby matures and develops so will pretend play and imitative play.

welcome to my world

Ages: 3 months and up

Explore your baby's world from their perspective: see what they see, touch what they touch, smell what they smell, hear what they hear. Pretend you're a baby too! What does that table look like underneath? How about the ceiling? Wow, is everything huge or what? Spend a day and take pictures as you experience baby's world. Take pictures of your child's favorite toys and stuffed animals. It will help your child remember what it was like to be a baby and who his special toys and friends were when he grows up. Put these pictures in a small photo album for baby to look at. Make up stories about baby's world.

84

★ Wit & Wisdom ★

When my daughter was three months old, her favorite toy was a brightly colored scarf. I could stuff it in my bag and take it anywhere, put Alice on her back and move the scarf up and down and side to side. She was entertained and I was able to visit with a friend without carting a bag of toys along.
—Jen W., Groveland, California

crawl space race

Ages: 6 months and up

Crawl together in a hallway or open area to capture a favorite object, or see a favorite person. Put a toy at the end of the hallway and partially cover it under a blanket as you encourage baby to find it. This game becomes more elaborate as baby grows. You can play stop and go, crawl behind baby trying to catch her tickling at her heels; or race to a location like the bathtub in the classic family favorite "last one in the bathtub is a silly pie," a "wet noodle," or a "rotten egg," ....you get the idea. This kind of fun is bound to make you laugh, and baby loves that sound!

★ Wit & Wisdom ★

When my nine-month-old son began to crawl, we put a wooden frame inside our brick fireplace and covered it with foam padding. I decorated it with fun fabric that I rotated with the season.
—Angela G., Scottsdale, Arizona

scarf magic

Ages: 6 months and up

Materials
Empty rectangular Kleenex box
Empty paper-towel cardboard tube
Colorful scarves or scraps of fabric

Tie the scarves or fabric together, end to end, and put them into the Kleenex box or cardboard tube leaving a small piece peeking out. Because of baby's curious nature, and busy hands, he will enjoy pulling the long scarf out of its hiding place. If he doesn't pull the scarf out by himself, show him how. Pull gently and say, "I'm pulling the scarf, now you pull." Baby will most likely want to pull the scarves out a few times in a row before moving on to something else. Once the scarves are out of the box or tube, wiggle them on the floor like a snake. Baby may like holding the scarf while crawling around the house.

pick which one

Ages: 6 months and up

Guessing games are always a favorite with babies. Play this one to keep baby entertained while she sits in her high chair in your kitchen or in restaurants. Put a piece of baby-safe peeled fruit like banana, melon, peach or apricot on baby's tray. Cover it with a plastic measuring bowl. Then, put one or two others bowls upside down on the tray and move them around. See if baby can pick the bowl with the fruit underneath. Play until she finds her treat, acting surprised when she picks a bowl with nothing under it as you ask the question, "Where is the fruit?"

★ Wit & Wisdom ★

My twelve-month-old loves taking my box of plastic cookie cutters and making shapes in the carpet. There is no mess, she can make different designs and learn how to handle and press the cutters with no messy dough.
—Hannah K., Norfolk, Virginia

croquet for crawlers

Ages: 9 months and up

Materials
Shoe boxes
Tennis ball

Cut the square ends off of a shoebox. Then cut the box into three sections that will stand on their own, those will be the wickets. First line the wickets up about get the idea. Ask baby to roll it back to you. As baby gets the hang of it space the wickets in any arrangement you like. Encourage baby to crawl to retrieve the ball and roll it back towards the wickets.

88

★ Wit & Wisdom ★
Don't forget the age-old jack-in-the-box toy. My six-month-old used to sit forever listening to the music as I cranked the metal arm waiting gleefully for the top to open. Each time she seemed completely surprised.
—Monica S., Arlington, VA.

off and on

Ages: 12 months and up

Babies love to take the covers off pots, pans, shoe boxes, salad spin-
ners, toothbrush holders, baby-wipe containers and anything else they
can get their hands on. Encourage baby's enthusiasm and newly
acquired fine motor skills by offering her lots of containers with lids to
play with. As baby gets older, you might even play a matching game.
Give her an equal amount of lids and containers then help her decides
what goes with what. Start with a few containers at first and increase
matching options as baby gets the hang of the game. If you are using
containers that look similar, try putting one sticker on the lid and a
matching one on the container. Another fun game uses containers with
twist-on lids. Put one of baby's toys inside and ask baby to help you
figure out how to get it out. Let baby problem-solve for a minute before
jumping in to rescue the toy. Praise baby's efforts with smiles and claps.

box of socks

Ages: 12 months and up

Materials
Laundry basket or box
Socks of different sizes

A box of old socks offers hours of entertainment. First let baby have fun trying them on and pulling them off. Try to choose loose-fitting socks, you know, the kind that don't require a crowbar to remove! When baby tires of trying the socks on, they may want to throw them in the air and watch them float to the floor. Roll the socks inside themselves to form softballs. You may want to put one strip of masking tape around the ball to help it stay in a ball shape. Start tossing the socks into the basket. Begin close to the basket and back up as baby gets better at making baskets. You can make a variety of games out of softball socks. Set up some plastic figures and roll the socks on the floor, or throw the ball trying to hit them. Throw the socks up in the air and catch them or roll them to each other.

fill and roll

Ages: 12 months and up

Materials
Clean oatmeal container with lid
Clear bottle or container with lid
Tennis balls, favorite stuffed animal, toy cars, or any object baby has
fun playing with that fits inside the oatmeal or clear container

Put whatever object you want inside the oatmeal container and put the
lid on. With baby in front of you, each of you roll the container on the
floor back and forth to each other. Say "what's inside?" and encourage
baby to take the top off and empty the container. Of course, many
babies need no encouragement and will peel the top off, empty the contents, and squeal with joy before you can blink! Another fun fill-and-roll
activity is to put something inside the clear container, roll it, and watch
the object inside twist and turn and the container rolls.

cheerio!

Ages: 12 months and up

When you first notice baby's interest in pouring, let her go for it. Provide paper cups with cereal, like Cheerios, empty egg cartons, or any other container into which they can pour. Babies love this work. Watch how they pinch and scoop the cereal into their cups. Of course, they will probably eat half the Cheerios, but that's half the fun! Make sure you feel comfortable with baby's oral-motor bite/chew skills before playing this game.

★ Wit & Wisdom ★

When my son was a little over a year we began sorting and stacking playing cards. A friend suggested that I turn the bottom of a shoebox over and cut inch-deep slots to slip the cards into either standing vertically or disappearing under the box. They also make a fun flapping sound when you run your hand over the top of them.
—Maggie S., West Bend, Wisconsin

wrap it up!

Ages: 12 months and up

Materials
Favorite baby toys: cars, blocks, Wiffle ball, cup, spoon, stuffed animal
Tissue paper or old wrapping paper
Tape

Every few weeks take one or two of baby's toys and put them away someplace where baby won't see them. Then bring the toys out and wrap them like presents in the tissue paper and place them near baby. Each bundle is fun for baby to unwrap, and if baby hasn't seen the toy for awhile baby may get excited as if it were new. A variation of this game is to partially hide the present so that baby has to look for it. Or perhaps establish a special place where you put gifts for baby. So when baby sees a wrapped present sitting in that particular location, he will know the gift is for him. Have plenty of tape ready. As you've probably learned by now, if something is fun for baby once, it is just as fun the second time.

★ **Wit & Wisdom** ★

I put my son's artwork in a three-ring binder, starting with his first scribble. His portfolio is now in its third volume and he looks at it often.
—Julia Y., Walnut Creek, California

93

my beautiful balloon

Ages: 12 months and up

Materials
Helium-filled Mylar balloons
String

Babies love balloons. They're colorful, lightweight, and magical. They seem to float and fly, which is what most babies believe they can do as well. Whether baby is crawling or walking, pulling something on a string is a grand lesson in cause and effect. Baby moves and the balloon moves along too. You take a turn at pulling the balloon, and ask baby to follow it. Remind baby to be gentle with the balloon.

Baby will also love to throw balloons in the air and watch them fall to the ground, and kick them around the room. They may even try sitting on them to pop them. Balloons are a lot of fun, but they are also dangerous so make sure to supervise closely and keep baby from putting the balloon in or around the mouth. Regular helium balloons can be used as well, but the Mylar ones are less dangerous when popped.

stack attack

Ages: 12 months and up

Materials
Wooden blocks (unit blocks, all sizes and shapes)

Begin to collect blocks now because their value is immeasurable and they will be used for years to come. They are fun to hold, carry, drop, stack, knock over, pull, push, and sort. With experience, baby will construct rows, simple bridges, enclosures, and patterns. Eventually blocks are transformed into food, animals, vehicles, boats, trains, planes, walls, roads, rivers, train tracks, buildings, furniture, tools, and mountains in baby's imagination.

Store blocks in a basket or plastic container where baby is able to reach them. Low, sturdy shelves are ideal for holding blocks and other favorite toys. As you explore blocks together, observe baby's choices. Use descriptive words, such as "smooth," "hard," "curved," "pointed," and "straight." Blocks never lose their value, and never go out of style.

tube slide

Ages: 15 months and up

Materials
Different sizes of cardboard tube, the longer the better
Small cars or balls

Balance one end of the tube on a couch, stool, or pillow. Put the other end of the tube on the ground so that the tube is angled downward like a slide. Put balls, cars, etc. in the tube at the top and watch them come out at the bottom. It is the disappearing and reappearing aspect of this activity that amuses baby. Even if baby can't hold the tube she will sit anxiously waiting for the outcome. Babies will do this for long periods of time, always amazed that the object comes out at the other end!

tub of delights

Ages: 18 months and up

Materials
Large plastic tub with cover, or shallow cardboard box with cover
Set of plastic or metal measuring cups
Funnel, strainer, ice cream scoop
One of the following: oatmeal, rice, cornmeal, birdseed

Pour one of the dried goods into the container. Sit on the floor, or stand around the child size table with baby and play in the tub. Use words to describe what you feel. For example, "This rice feels hard." As you fill, pour, and stir, continue to give baby words for what is happening. It is fun to hide small plastic toys in the dried goods, so as baby digs around, surprises are found. Touch, like all baby's senses, gives baby valuable information about the world. This is a good in or outdoor activity. Outside it is an alternative to the sandbox, and if you use something like birdseed or oatmeal you can leave the mess on the floor for the birds to eat.

make me a match

Materials
Masking tape
Laundry basket or box
Things in sets of two: coasters, paper napkins, gloves, large earrings, socks, spoons, shoes, etc.

Create a trail with masking tape on the floor. Use as much floor space as possible. Make a large square shape on the floor with masking tape at the end of the trail to put the found matches in. Place one item from each matching set somewhere along the trail, and keep the other matching item in the basket at the beginning of the trail. Together you and baby pick an object from the basket and say, "Let's go find the same." Do one match at a time, setting the pair in the box at the end of your trail. Go back to the beginning and pick something else out of the box. As baby gets better understanding the concept of matching, you can try using objects that are the same but not identical, for instance two different pairs of shoes.

movement

massage

Ages: 0 and up
(as soon as umbilical cord has healed)

Materials
Blanket or towel
Pure vegetable oil
Soft music (optional)

Make sure the room is warm before beginning. Sit with your back against a couch, with legs stretched straight in front. Place a towel on top of your legs, then put baby on top of the towel. You may need to put a small pillow from knee to foot so baby isn't sliding downward. Now, take baby's clothes off, leaving diaper on if necessary. Pour a small amount of oil into your hand, about the size of a quarter. Rub your hands together until the oil and your hands feel warm. Talk to baby as you gently but firmly place hands, palms down, on baby's chest. Rub from chest down to toes, from chest out to fingertips, as many times as you like. Make sure to rub slowly. Gently hold hand or foot, and using small thumb strokes, massage palm of hand or bottom of foot. Turn baby over and massage back. It doesn't really matter your massage style; what is most important is eye contact, your voice, and your feeling of love. As baby gets older, you might try singing a song announcing each body part, like "Hi ho the derio, I'm rubbing Sally's feet."

stretching

Ages: 0 and up (as soon as umbilical cord has healed)

Sit in a comfortable place with baby lying on a flat, soft surface. Sing, talk, or play music baby likes. Hold both of baby's arms out to the side. Grasp the wrists, then gently bring each arm to cross over baby's chest and hold for a few seconds, then return to baby's side. Bend and straighten each arm, then stretch both arms over baby's head. Hold baby's left hand with your right hand and baby's right foot with your left hand. Bring hand and foot to cross each other. Hold for a few seconds. Repeat on other side. Put baby's legs in cross-legged fashion and raise knees up towards stomach. Hold. Smile at baby and talk to baby about what you are doing. Say "Stretch, stretch, stretch those cute little legs." Baby loves your voice and may even smile. Stretching is especially important when baby cannot move by herself yet.

★ **Wit & Wisdom** ★

The only time my daughter, who had colic, would stop crying was when I was massaging her. It must have alleviated some of the gas in her stomach.
—Charlotte H., Washington, D.C.

dancing the night away

Ages: 3 months and up

Materials
Your voice
Radio, cassette/CD player, or stereo

Move any object that might trip someone, making enough room to move in all directions. Everyone can dance, just let yourself go. Hold your baby tight, turn on the music and move. Lift baby up and down, turning around and around, lift left and right, step forward and back. If the room isn't large enough, don't confine yourself, move from room to room. Dancing of all kinds will gain new meaning as baby grows from moving in your arms to following your rhythm and dancing on her own.

Another fun dance is the wiggle and shake. Put the music on and starting with your fingertips, arms, and shoulders begin to shake and wiggle. Move from one body part to the next. Baby will laugh just watching you. As baby gets older she will be able to wiggle along with you. Wiggle your hands up and down baby's body or on each other's backs or arms.

tummy time

Ages: 3 months and up

Spending a little time each day on her tummy will help baby strengthen the back, shoulders and neck muscles in preparation for sitting and crawling. Don't force baby to stay in this position for more than a few seconds if she doesn't like it, but try a few of these ideas to keep baby entertained as she strengthens!

- Get on the floor yourself across from baby so that you are face to face. Make funny expressions or blow softly, puffing your cheeks out.
- Place a colorful toy with moving parts in front of baby.
- When baby is around six months old you can get behind baby, putting a rolled-up towel at baby's feet, and encourage baby to push against the towel and inch forward.
- Place a mirror on the right side six inches away from baby's face. Move the mirror around the front and over to the other side, encouraging baby to turn her head to the other side.
- Your encouraging voice and smiling face is baby's best motivator.

morning exercise

Ages: 6 months and up

Take some time to do some simple exercises together. You may be getting more exercise than baby, but baby has a whole lifetime to get in shape!

- Baby lies on floor on stomach, the adult lies on stomach face to face with baby. Adult does push-up, and as adult goes up, baby exercises neck muscles by raising head to look.
- Adult lies on side to do leg lifts. Baby lies on back in front of adult. As adult lifts leg, adult puts hand on baby's stomach and moves baby side to side in a rolling motion.
- Adult lies on back to do stomach curls. Baby lies on adult's chest, stomach to stomach. Adult slowly raises up and down tightening stomach muscles. Baby enjoys the ride up and down.
- Adult sits in straddle position with baby lying on baby's back between adults legs with head facing out ward. Let baby grasp index finger or thumb with her hands then let baby pull up slowly being careful not to let baby fall backwards. As baby lies back down, adult stretches forward.

★ Wit & Wisdom ★

My son loves to be rolled on top of a big ball. I hold him securely as he lies over the top and I rock him back and forth.
—Samantha F., Austin, Texas

go get it

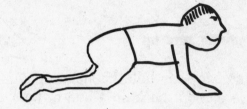

Ages: 6 months and up

Materials
Balls of all sizes
Stuffed animals or toys

Whether your baby walks, crawls, or runs, he will like this game of exercise and fun. Throw a ball or toy a few feet ahead of you for him to go and get. Have him bring it back to you or to a bucket as quickly as he can. There are all sorts of variations on this that will depend on your baby's age and development stage. You can throw many things at once and tell him the order he has to pick them up. You can throw two colored balls and ask him to get the red one. Baby can throw the ball or toy for you to go and get, or the two of you could race to get it. The main idea is for both of you to run or crawl around having fun.

baby flying

Ages: 6 months and up

As soon as baby can hold his head up, you can play all sorts of flying games. Lie on your back on a bed or floor and holding baby's armpits, lift him up and down, side to side, dipping like a plane, swerving in the air as you make plane sounds. Tell baby he is flying up in the air.

- Place baby on the floor, stomach down, as you stand above baby with a foot on either side. Hold baby with both your hands under the stomach and swing, back and forth and side to side. Make sure you are bending your knees so you don't hurt your back.
- Hold your baby tummy down, with your arm under her chest and belly, like you are carrying a football. This position is calming for most babies. In this position imitate a plane flying, swing baby back and forth, dipping low, circling one way and then the other.
- Another great swinging game for the older baby (about twelve months) is to take one hand and one foot and swing them round in a circle. You can play this with baby face up or face down. This truly feels like flying, gliding up and down as they fly around the circle.

mirror dance

Ages: 9 months and up

Begin the dance by facing each other. The best way to teach baby how to mirror someone is to mirror what baby does, copying the movements. Whatever movement baby makes, you do the same thing at the same time. Raise your arms, touch your nose, mess up your hair, or do whatever you think baby is capable of doing back. The older the baby the more dance-like the interaction will become.

follow me

Ages: 12 months and up

Materials
Backyard/living room
Several cushions
Laundry basket
Favorite toy/ball
Jump rope
Cardboard box
Mattress

Use the interesting items above to design an obstacle course. Once set up, you lead the way using the various forms of locomotion your baby has been working so hard to master. Begin with walking or crawling forward, then backward, squatting, and turning. Perhaps your child likes to jump, walk on tip-toe, or roll. You can use the rope as a straight line to direct baby where she should walk to next. When baby is first starting to pull herself up, or toddling with the first steps it helps to have large objects she can push across the floor. So fill the laundry basket with a few toys or old magazines and help baby get the idea of pushing by pulling the laundry basket from the other side, showing baby that the basket will move forward if she pushes. Include this as part of the obstacle course.

simon says

Ages: 12 months and up

Here is a variation to the usual Simon Says game. Instead of leaving the words "Simon says" out once in a while in hopes of tricking baby to mess up, leave the words "Simon says" in all the time. This then becomes a simple game of doing what you say or imitating what you do. You can also add more exercise oriented activities, like "Simon says run around the room two times," or "Simon says bicycle your legs." If baby is too young to do the movements on his own, you can step in and lift the arms or bicycle the legs.

walk and find

Ages: 12 months and up

Once baby has discovered the joy of walking the few steps from couch to ottoman to chair, add a little fun to the action by placing a favorite toy wherever you think the next stopping point might be. Once baby gets the idea that you are placing the toy as bait to get him to walk to the next location, he will smile and toddle as fast as he can to wherever you place the toy. When baby understands the game, let baby see you hide a toy under a cushion or behind a chair. As baby gets older, you can hide the object in the general area and let baby look for it on his own.

★ Wit & Wisdom ★

My daughter's absolute favorite game, she called "flashlight jump." I'd shine a flashlight on the floor and she would try to crawl, walk, or jump to where the light was. Once she got there, I'd move the light to another location and she'd race toward the light. I started this game when she became afraid of the dark; having fun in the dark really helped her get over the fear.
—Karen C., Alameda, California

scarf scuffle

Ages: 12 months and up

Materials
Chiffon scarves
Music

Clear any obstacles out of the room, or go outside. Give your child a few scarves and begin to throw them into the air. Watch them float down to the ground. Imitate the scarf movements with your body. Drape the scarves around your bodies and dance, imagining you are clouds, birds, ballerinas, or leaves. Use your imagination and enjoy the soft, graceful, floating movements.

leaf stomp

Ages: 15 months and up

Babies are mesmerized with leaves in the fall. They love to watch them float down to the ground, the color draws their attention, and the crunching sound they make when stepped on is irresistible. Find a large box. Cut the sides of the box so they are about 15 inches from the ground. You want the sides of the box to be tall enough so baby's hands can rest on them for balance. Fill the bottom of the box with leaves. Put baby in the box on top of the leaves, making sure to hold onto the box so it won't tip over. Encourage baby to stomp on the leaves. When the crunching stops, dump the leaves out and begin again. When finished, rake up a pile of leaves and jump into it.

big swings

Ages: 18 months and up

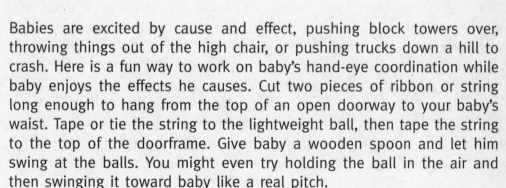

Materials
Ribbon or string
Lightweight ball

Babies are excited by cause and effect, pushing block towers over, throwing things out of the high chair, or pushing trucks down a hill to crash. Here is a fun way to work on baby's hand-eye coordination while baby enjoys the effects he causes. Cut two pieces of ribbon or string long enough to hang from the top of an open doorway to your baby's waist. Tape or tie the string to the lightweight ball, then tape the string to the top of the doorframe. Give baby a wooden spoon and let him swing at the balls. You might even try holding the ball in the air and then swinging it toward baby like a real pitch.

art and
sculpture

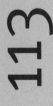

the art's in the doing

Ages: 3 months and up

What "art" can a baby make? Well, to begin with, you and baby will create together. Then, as baby grows, is able to hold a marker or paintbrush, and learns through experience that not everything is edible, the art experience will change. Some things that do not change are: you must offer the appropriate supplies, model the use of various tools, closely supervise, facilitate baby's exploration, and clean up. Always remember that process is more important than the final product! Take a few minutes and remember some of your earliest art experiences. What materials did you use? Do you remember how you felt? What was your favorite form of expression? As you approach each new art experience with baby, enjoy yourself, and allow baby to show you what "artistic freedom" really means.

★ **Wit & Wisdom** ★

I found a great way to save my son's drawings.
I simply glue them onto an old calendar.
—Ian P., Sedona, AZ

first paintings

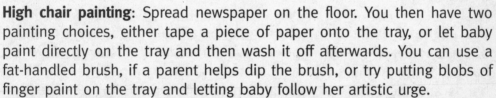

Ages: 6 months and up

Babies love the feel of paint, the bright colors, and the freedom of spreading it across various surfaces. Here are three fun painting experiments.

High chair painting: Spread newspaper on the floor. You then have two painting choices, either tape a piece of paper onto the tray, or let baby paint directly on the tray and then wash it off afterwards. You can use a fat-handled brush, if a parent helps dip the brush, or try putting blobs of finger paint on the tray and letting baby follow her artistic urge.

Pudding painting: This form of painting is for those babies who can't keep their hands out of their mouths and so need a form of paint that is digestible. Mix up a batch of vanilla instant pudding. Divide the pudding into bowls adding a drop or two of food color to each bowl. Follow the steps in high chair painting above.

Naked body on butcher paper: Babies love sliding, squishing, and smearing finger paint. Why not give them a chance to use their entire body? First, tape a few long sheets of butcher paper together to make a 10 feet by 10 feet square (or use an old sheet taped to the floor). Take off baby's clothes. Pour blobs of finger paint onto the paper or sheet. Let baby spread paint around however he chooses. Have the bath or wading pool ready!

hands of love

Ages: 9 months and up

Materials
Liquid tempera paint (any color) or acrylic paint
Plastic tray, cookie sheet, or lid of rectangular tub
Several sheets of heavy-weight drawing paper or finger painting paper
Paintbrush

Use paints to paint baby's hands or feet. Then press them onto the paper and let dry. Add a border with a marker or crayon. Date the hand/foot prints and save them. As baby grows, compare her little baby hands and feet with her "big girl" hand/foot prints. You can also use acrylic paint and do hand/foot prints on fabric of any kind. Hand-printed T-shirts, aprons, handbags, and sheets make great holiday or birthday presents.

★ Wit & Wisdom ★
After trying many stain removers on my kids' dirty clothes, I discovered that liquid dishwasher detergent, if left to sit for ten minutes before washing, worked every time.
—Stacey T., Houston, Texas

watercolor

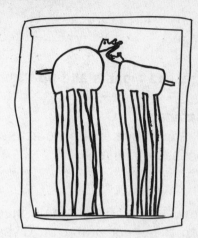

Ages: 9 months and up

Materials
Watercolor paint (the kind you get
  at the grocery store in a plastic case)
Paper
Paintbrush
Crayons

Watercolor is easy and fun. Make sure to buy a huge paintbrush instead of using the one that comes with most watercolor paint sets. Get a dish full of water, and show baby how to dip the paintbrush into the water, then the paint. It's also fun to do a crayon drawing on the paper first, then paint over the top and the crayon will show through. You may want to let baby paint many sheets of paper to be used throughout the year as note cards, stationery, or wrapping paper. Another fun watercolor project is to get a piece of butcher paper longer than baby. Ask baby to lie on the paper so you can outline baby's body. Then have baby paint over her body outline, adding clothes, or just colorful design work.

mark and erase pictures

Ages: 12 months and up

Materials
Plastic sleeve sheet protectors
Washable markers
White paper

Draw simple designs on a piece of white paper. Slip the piece of paper into the sheet protector. Give baby the markers and let baby draw on top, trying to follow the simple lines or making a design of his own. When baby finishes, simply wipe off the plastic to erase the drawing and begin again. This is a great activity to do when you're visiting someone who doesn't have baby or art supplies, or when waiting for food in a restaurant.

tea party dough

Ages: 12 months and up

Materials
A mixing bowl
1 cup peanut butter
1 cup corn syrup
1½ cups powdered sugar
1½ cups powdered milk

Mix ingredients together in the bowl. Additional powdered milk may be needed to make the dough not so sticky. Knead. Use cookie cutters or design your own shapes. If the tea party idea doesn't fly, try having a birthday party. Birthday candles are fun to stick in dough.

You might also give baby the lump of dough and see what kind of sculpture she designs. Show her how to roll long, thin tubes. Make the dough into smaller balls and pile them on top of each other to make a tower. Or just squeeze the dough enjoying the feel of dough between fingers. Make sure to taste it!

contact collage

Ages: 12 months and up

Materials
1 roll of clear contact paper
Magazine pictures of children, animals,
  toys, nature, etc.
Small pieces of fabric: felt, burlap, velvet,
  corduroy, or denim
Scissors
Tape

Cut a large piece of contact paper and tape it to the floor or at baby's eye level on the wall with the backing facing up. Then peel off the backing (peel around the tape). Cut pictures from magazines and a variety of fabric shapes. Pick a picture or piece of material and place it on the sticky contact paper. Let baby choose which pieces, and observe and talk about her choices using descriptive phrases such as, "You chose a picture of a red ball."

crumple crazy

Ages: 12 months and up

Materials
White tissue paper (other colors are great, but dyes will transfer
  onto hands when tissue is wet)
Cardboard: cereal box, posterboard, or construction paper
Glue

Add one teaspoon water and two tablespoons glue together in a small
container. Cut or tear tissue paper into small pieces. Crumple tissue
paper. Squeeze or brush some glue onto the cardboard and "hide" the
glue with crumpled tissue paper. Baby may decide to simply tear and
crumple. Then again, baby might want to squeeze glue onto the cardboard until it resembles a small puddle. You can also use a glue stick,
but the tissue doesn't stick as easily. You may also want to divide up
the jobs and let baby rip the tissue paper and scrunch it into small balls
while you do the gluing.

the scribble

Ages: 12 months and up

Materials
Large paper (experiment with different types)
Large nontoxic watercolor markers
Large crayons

When baby draws and scribbles, something new is created. What joy there is in being able to express thoughts and feelings in this way, not to mention the pure pleasure of using the materials! Baby can begin to scribble as soon as he can hold a crayon in his hand. Put the paper on the floor or a low table that has been covered with newspaper. It also works to tape the paper to the refrigerator front at baby's eye level. A long sheet of butcher paper is also a great way to start, giving baby lots of room. Place the markers or crayons in a tray next to the paper. Make sure to say, "The markers are for drawing on the paper." Sit and draw with baby. Save some drawings each month, and make a book for baby's birthday each year. This is a great way to "see" creativity grow and develop.

★ Wit & Wisdom ★

Remove crayon marks from wallpaper with a hairdryer set on hot. First, the wax heats up, then it can be wiped off with a damp cloth and oil soap.
—Jared S., Foster City, California

musical chalk

Ages: 15 months and up

Materials
Sidewalk chalk
Masking tape
Large pieces of paper
Liquid starch
Small paintbrush

Play music you love while baby makes his chalk dance on paper. Wrap one end of the chalk with masking tape. This cuts down on the amount of chalk on baby's hands. Tape paper to a work surface: refrigerator, child-size table, or floor. Play music. Say, "Listen to the music" and "Let's make our chalk dance on the paper." Work with dry chalk on dry paper initially. Once baby has some chalk experience, use dry chalk and paper brushed with a light coat of liquid starch. Another method is to leave the paper dry and dip the chalk into a small container of starch. The chalk must be dipped several times with this last technique. The larger the paper the better, since it gives baby freedom to use whole arm movements, which is exactly what baby needs.

sandpaper line designs

Ages: 15 months and up

Materials
Coarse sandpaper
Yarn of any kind

Cut the yarn into several different lengths, using as much or as little as you want. Different textures and colors will make the picture more interesting. Pick up the yarn and put a piece on the sandpaper, showing baby how it's done. The yarn will stick to the sandpaper as you and baby create designs together. If you want to change your designs, go ahead—simply move the yarn. Put these reusable materials in a Ziploc bag. Wherever you are, this is a quiet, clean art experience.

★ **Wit & Wisdom** ★
I see, and I remember,
I do, and I understand.
—Chinese proverb

stained glass window

Ages: 15 months and up

Materials
Assorted colored cellophane
Scissors
Tape
Strips of cardboard

Use long strips of cardboard to outline a large frame. Tape the frame to the window. Cut the cellophane into small two- to three-inch squares or different shapes. Have baby hold the piece of cellophane up to the window as you tape it on within the frame. Add many pieces until a large square is made that resembles a stained glass window. As light shines through the window, enjoy the color and design. As baby gets older, you might want to make a design. Use a washable marker to draw the picture on the glass window, then have baby help you decide what colors of cellophane to color the picture in with.

blob painting

Ages: 15 months and up

Materials
2 to 3 small plastic cosmetic bottles (the travel
  kind) or large plastic droppers used to give
  baby's liquid medicine
Tempera paint
Paper, paper towels, or coffee filters

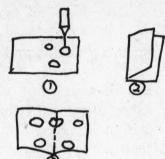

Put a different color of paint into each bottle or pour paint into bowls and suck up paint into the dropper. Baby can squeeze the paint himself onto the paper in small puddles. Once many small puddles are on the paper, fold the paper in half and rub lightly over the top, causing a print to be made.

It is also fun to put blobs of paint all over one piece of paper, then put another piece of paper over the top, and rub. Paper towels or coffee filters are also great to use because the paint will spread out and run together. When using coffee filters or paper towels you won't need to fold them in half, just drop the blobs onto the paper and watch them spread.

pipe cleaner sculpture

Ages: 15 months and up

Buy a bag of colored pipe cleaners. Show baby how to bend and move them. Work together to create a sculpture, attaching one pipe cleaner to the next. Make a chain of pipe cleaners with a small designed pipe-cleaner sculpture hanging at the end.

Show baby how the sculpture you are making moves by holding onto two ends of the sculpture and moving back and forth. Maybe it looks like a dog walking down the street or a clown laughing. Make up stories about your sculptures.

★ Wit & Wisdom ★

My daughter hated to wear hats. Because she had fair skin, she had no choice. One day, I decided to put a hat rack up for her and buy a few different sun hats. I hung it in her room and now that she gets to choose one each day, she gladly wears them.
—Silvia T., Daytona, Florida

a box is a box

Ages: 18 months and up

Materials
Any size box with staples removed
Liquid tempera paint
Paintbrush or small sponge paint roller
Newspapers or drop cloth

A box is a box until baby paints it. Then it's a beautiful craft and imaginative toy! If you can suspend disbelief, your box transforms many times over: into a garage, mailbox, cave, house, railroad station, castle, boat, and yes, even a hat. Spread the drop cloth or newspapers on the ground to make cleanup easier and to define the workspace. Put ¼ cup paint in a sturdy plastic container or tray. Put the box on the newspaper and set the paintbrush close. See what baby does with the brush before you put it into the paint. You may decide to use two brushes so that you can paint at the same time as baby. Hold the paint container so it won't spill as baby haphazardly dips the brush. Expect a little mess and dress accordingly.

butterfly art

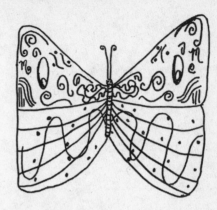

Ages: 18 months and up

Materials
Thick, absorbent paper towel
Watercolor paints
Pipe cleaner
Eyedropper

Lay the paper towel out on the table. Use the dropper to drop water-color paints all over the paper towel. Watch as the liquid spreads out, making a creative design. Scrunch the paper towel in the middle, gathering in the paper to form the butterfly body. Use the leftover pipe cleaner to form antennae and voilà, a beautiful butterfly! Make many butterflies. Take colored pieces of string and hang them high up next to the ceiling for a breath of spring any time of the year.

toys and games

black and white pictures

Ages: 0 and up

Materials
White paper
Black markers

Newborn babies are attracted to the sharply contrasting colors of black and white. They also like the bold patterns of diagonals, bull's-eyes, and checkerboards. The human face is a favorite of all babies. Take the white paper and make a simple face with hair, eyebrows, eyes, nose, and mouth. Make some other patterns. Tape your masterpieces to the inside of the crib, the bassinet, or the car window. Babies see best seven to nine inches from their face.

baby watch games

Ages: 0 to 3 months

- Find or buy many pretty colored ribbons. Attach the ribbons to a stick and wave the stick in front of baby making short, jerky motions as well as long, looping motions.

- Play swat the toy. Tie a long shoestring to a small stuffed toy. Swing the toy in front of baby and let baby try to reach for it as the toy slowly swings past.

- Buy a pinwheel and stick it in a houseplant, out in the garden, or someplace breezy where baby can watch it.

- Tie a robe across the top of a crib or playpen. Use large clothespins and attach various toys to the robe. Change the toys regularly.

★ Wit & Wisdom ★

Encourage baby to chew on safe teething toys. This is how baby explores the world and his environment. Mouthing different textured toys will introduce the concepts of hard, soft, bumpy, and smooth textures prior to introducing food textures.
—Martha S., Salt Lake City, Utah

mobiles

Ages: 0 to 6 months

Materials
Embroidery hoop, hanger, or pie tin
Heavy-weight string or yarn
Assorted household objects or small stuffed animals
Ceiling hook

The idea of a mobile is to hang household objects from the hanger, pie tin, or embroidery hoop. The mobile is then hung from the ceiling by a hook. Here are a few ideas to get you started.

1. Light mobile: take pieces of cardboard, cut into different shapes, and cover them with aluminum foil. When the light from a window hits the foil, the light will reflect around the room.
2. Hang small, brightly colored boxes that food comes in.
3. Hang small stuffed animals or figures face down so baby can look up and see them.
4. Hang small jingle bells, or other things that make a musical sound when the wind hits them.

When baby is old enough to reach up and touch, or pull on the hanging objects, the mobile should be removed and more age-appropriate toys should be introduced.

personal picture book

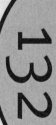

Ages: 6 months and up

Materials
Photo albums with adhesive pages
Photos of family, friends, pets, food,
  nature, toys, clothes, etc.

Make up a few books of your own for
baby to look at. Since baby doesn't read, simply tell a different story
each time you look at the pictures together. Use people and objects that
baby can see in his everyday world. Talk about and describe what the
people are doing. Point out the way things function and how they are
used daily. You may even walk to the object or person in the house and
hold up the picture and say "same."

Put only one picture per page, so baby is not confused with what you
are talking about. Use magazines, greeting cards, and catalogs as well
as your own photos. It would also be fun to make a book using only
pictures of baby.

new switch-it game

Ages: 6 months and up

Babies love to hold, grasp, and squeeze everything from earrings to keys to mom's hair. Take advantage of baby's curious nature. Place baby on your lap, then hold a toy out in front of him. Once baby has the toy in his hand, hold another one just within reach out in front of that same hand. Watch as baby tries to figure out what he is going to do with the toy he is already holding and doesn't really want to let go of. Sometimes baby will just drop the toy he is holding, but after a while baby will figure out how to switch the toy to the other hand so that both toys can be held at the same time.

★ **Wit & Wisdom** ★

My baby used to love it when I'd turn off the light and shine a flashlight behind some toy or action figure. I would move the toy forward and back and he'd watch wide-eyed as the shadows would grow and shrink.
—Nadine W., Ann Arbor, Michigan

textured touch

Ages: 9 months and up

Materials
Assorted textured pieces: velvet, silk, terry cloth, burlap,
 leather, fake fur, corduroy, sandpaper
Flat box with lid (tie or scarf boxes work well)

Take the thin box and punch two finger holes in the top next to each other. Put a textured piece in the box. Show baby how to put a finger in the box and feel the texture, then put your finger in the box and play with baby's finger as you both feel the textured piece. Make sure to put words to the textures you are feeling: smooth, rough, silky, fuzzy, soft, or hard. As baby gets older, you can put the textured pieces as well as other objects in a paper bag one at a time and have baby guess what is in the bag.

★ Wit & Wisdom ★

Take an old rubber suction soap dish, thoroughly cleaned, and give it to baby for teething. Also, the suction cups can be put on things within baby's reach, such as the refrigerator. They will love to pull it off and hear the suction pop.
—Jan C., Edina, Minnesota

finger puppet play

Ages: 12 months and up

Materials
Old gloves
Colored felt pieces
Paint pens
Needle and thread

Cut the fingers off the glove, and sew the cut edge under ½ inch to prevent unraveling. Cut the felt pieces to make ears, nose, hat, whiskers, arms, etc. Using fabric pens, make faces and add detail. Make up stories about the puppets and give them names. Play hide-and-seek, making the puppets disappear under a pillow or behind a doll. Wear them on your fingers and when baby gets bored, wiggle them around close to baby making funny sounds!

If you don't want to construct individual finger puppets, use the fabric pens to make faces on each finger of the glove and use your whole hand.

There are a variety of inexpensive finger puppets available at stores. These are great to collect, stick in your purse, and use to entertain baby anytime.

dropping games

Ages: 12 months and up

Materials
Large container that has smooth
  edges when the lid is removed
Clothespins (the kind that you
  don't have to pinch to open)
Balls
Toys

Clothespin fun: Stand above the container and drop the clothespins in, or stand two to three feet away and try to toss the clothespins in.
Sit next to the container on the floor and slip the clothespins around the top. Then take them off and put them on again. Put the clothespins inside the container, then put the plastic lid back on and place the container on the floor and roll it around.

Balls, socks, toys: Babies love to watch things fall. Try dropping whatever baby can find into the container. Stand on a stool to watch it drop further. Baby especially likes to drop things onto the floor as he sits in his high chair. Make a game out of this by giving baby a container of things that can be safely dropped on the floor.

games with balls

Ages: 12 months and up

Homemade Paper Balls: Made by scrunching wadded-up paper into balls and wrapping masking tape around the outside, holding the crunched edges together. Roll the ball on the floor, trying to knock something over, or throw it into a box. Play catch or kick the ball. Baby may come up with a game or two of her own. The good news is that paper ball games can be played inside!

Hit the Target: Attach Velcro pieces to the homemade balls or Ping-Pong balls. Cut large targets in whatever shapes baby likes out of felt: circles, triangle, moon, or bear. Tape or glue the shapes onto a piece of cardboard, the side of a box, or directly onto the wall. Take aim and throw the balls at the target trying to get them to stick.

kitchen boxes

Ages: 12 months and up

Collect small boxes that food comes in, the smaller and brighter the better. Make sure the box is clean, then stuff the box with wadded up newspaper to help it keep its shape. Tape it shut with thick tape that won't peel off. When baby is very little, stack them up like blocks, but as soon as they start watching you work in the kitchen, they will want to copy you!

Set up a mini kitchen for them using larger cardboard boxes or an old hutch. Whenever you are tempted to throw away measuring cups, spoons, or pans donate them to baby's kitchen. Garage sales are a great place to find make-believe kitchen toys. Go together on a Saturday to search for pans, aprons, tea sets, and plastic food.

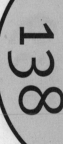

blowing games

Ages: 12 months and up

Blowing a variety of horns, bubbles, or party noise-makers is a great oral-motor activity for baby. Lip-rounding activities such as blowing naturally strengthen the tongue and mouth in preparation for clear speech. Play imitation games with the horns. First, you blow the horn one or two toots and then give baby the chance to answer. Watch the party horns roll in and out. Since they are soft, you could blow your rolling paper horn softly to unroll and touch baby's tummy.

ball in balloon

Ages: 12 months and up

Materials
Small rubber ball (the size of a golf ball)
Clear or light-colored thick rubber balloon

Begin by stretching the balloon over the rubber ball. Once the rubber ball is inside the balloon, blow up the balloon. Make sure the balloon is not blown so tightly that it will pop upon baby's touch.

Hold the balloon and show baby how the ball inside rolls around. Make the ball twirl and bounce inside the balloon. Drop the balloon to the ground and watch it hop up and down. Be very careful to watch baby with the balloon. Balloons are a choking hazard.

classic games

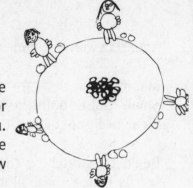

Ages: 12 months and up

Follow the Leader: Follow the Leader can be played many ways. You might just take a step or two forward and encourage baby to follow you. Maybe you notice something baby is doing, like crawling under a table, and you decide to follow him.

Patty-Cake: Hold your baby's hands at first and walk him through the motions. Once baby begins to anticipate the sounds and actions, he will do the patty-caking himself. Be creative and make up a few of your own verses.

Where's Your Nose?: Around a year old, baby becomes more aware of his body. Asking questions that baby can answer by pointing to his body is fun, interactive, and gives baby a feeling of accomplishment. Ask baby, "Where is baby's nose?" Then "Where is Mommy or Daddy's nose?" Repeat with other body parts.

match my picture

Ages: 15 months and up

Whenever you buy new toys, be sure to save a picture of them, either off the side of the box or from the catalog you ordered them from. If you don't have the exact picture, try to find one that looks similar. Hide (but not too much out of sight) the real objects that match the pictures. Then give baby one picture at a time and help her search the room to find the item that matches the picture.

Baby might also like to hide the objects while you shut your eyes and then give you one picture at a time so you have to find the objects. Make sure to make the search look difficult so baby will feel delight when you finally find the hidden object.

music

foot and hand jingles

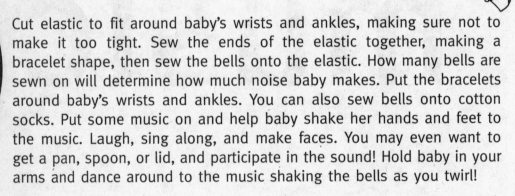

Ages: 0 and up

Materials
¼" elastic
Bells of any kind

Cut elastic to fit around baby's wrists and ankles, making sure not to make it too tight. Sew the ends of the elastic together, making a bracelet shape, then sew the bells onto the elastic. How many bells are sewn on will determine how much noise baby makes. Put the bracelets around baby's wrists and ankles. You can also sew bells onto cotton socks. Put some music on and help baby shake her hands and feet to the music. Laugh, sing along, and make faces. You may even want to get a pan, spoon, or lid, and participate in the sound! Hold baby in your arms and dance around to the music shaking the bells as you twirl!

★ Wit & Wisdom ★

When we were in the process of moving, I decided to sew bells onto my daughter's socks. I figured the movers and other adults moving in and out were less likely to accidentally walk into her as they carried heavy boxes.
—Susan W., Miami, Florida

143

baby's song

Ages: 6 months and up

Write a song describing some things baby does each day. You may want to write a wake-up song, a naptime song, a changing or eating song, and a bedtime lullaby. They might go something like this:

Wesley likes to take a bath, take a bath, take a bath.
Wesley likes to take a bath early every evening.
Wesley likes to splash around, splash around, splash around
Wesley likes to splash around as Mommy sponges water.

Pick any familiar melody or make one up. Most important, when baby hears his own name repeated over and over he feels he is in a safe, familiar place. Every time you do the activity, sing the song. This may even help baby identify and form patterns of behavior. For instance, if the same song is sung before naptime every day, just hearing the song might make baby tired. Now that is worth a try!

baby babble

Ages: 6 months and up

Listen to baby babble. There is sometimes a rhythm to the words or sounds. Baby may repeat the same sound melodically over and over. Once a pattern is detected, hum along or say the words baby is saying. Even singing "la, la, la" to baby's gurgling is song-like. Any sound baby makes is active communication. Take advantage of baby's efforts by joining in. Baby will be delighted and feel important at the same time.

★ Wit & Wisdom ★

Some pointers I learned about singing to my baby: First, don't stick to baby songs because they get boring. Second, use props to act out the song or move to the beat of the music. Last, have fun moving your voice up and down to the highest and lowest pitches. And no matter how much fun your older kids make of you, always make up your own lyrics, especially when you don't know the words.
—Michelle J., Chicago, Illinois

clapping games

Ages: 9 months and up

The object of clapping games is to use your own hands to make noise, to create repetitive interactive patterns, or to be your own rhythm section in the band. Begin by making up a repetitive clapping pattern. You might start by slapping your knees, then clapping twice. See if baby will copy you. Then let baby make up his own pattern and you copy.

Next, try to do the clapping pattern at the same time, perhaps clapping each other's hands. Then try making up a clapping dance beat and encourage baby to dance or move to your clapping rhythm. Try dancing along with baby as you clap.

music is hiding

Ages: 6 months and up

Wind up a musical toy baby likes and hide it somewhere in the room under a small blanket that is visible to baby. Make sure it is close enough so baby can hear it clearly. Ask baby "Where is the music?" Crawl around the room together looking for the music. If baby is old enough, have him hide the toy while you shut your eyes, and then look for the toy. Baby will be full of giggles if he hides the toy and you make a big deal of finding it (not right away, of course!).

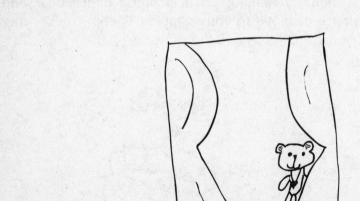

147

your child's voice

Ages: 9 months and up

Materials
Tape recorder
Cassette tape

Put a cassette tape in the tape recorder and give a little spoken introduction about your baby: age, date, things baby likes to do, baby's favorite foods, personality traits, etc. Record your child's voice, laughing, crying, babbling, and breathing. Sing songs, clap hands, and do whatever you do together each day. Plan on adding to this tape periodically so that baby can hear the music of her own voice over time.

rhythm sticks

Ages: 9 months and up

Materials
Lengths of wood doweling 6 to 8 inches long by ½ to 1 inch diameter
 (most lumber stores will cut the doweling to your specifications)
Sandpaper
High gloss acrylic paint

Sand the ends of the dowels until smooth. Paint the rhythm sticks in a variety of bright colors. Let them dry completely before using. Dowels can also be left a natural wood color by staining them. Make sure that anything put on the dowels is nontoxic. There are many games to play with rhythm sticks. Below are a few starting at three months old.

- Hum a melody while you tap the sticks together lightly.
- As baby begins to hold things, let him hold one in each hand as you hold one in each hand. Do a made-up patty-cake-type tapping.
- If the sticks are painted colors, match color to color as you hit them.
- Put on a music tape and tap together.
- Imitate baby's actions and encourage baby to imitate you.

Caution: Never leave baby alone with sticks. Never allow a newly walking child to hold on to sticks while they walk.

picture this, sing that

Ages: 9 months and up

Draw or find pictures that represent your favorite songs. For example
bus wheels for "The Wheels on the Bus," a spider for "Itsy, Bitsy
Spider," farm animals for "Old MacDonald Had a Farm." Laminate them.
Whenever you sing the song, hold up the laminated picture. Next, offer
baby two pictures and encourage him to choose which song will be
sung. Once baby gets used to picking the pictures he may reach for one
from the pile for you to sing.

drum time

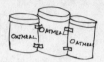

Ages: 12 months and up

Bongo Drums: All you need for bongos is three different sizes of oatmeal cylinders (cut them down to make them different sizes) and masking tape. Tape the cylinders together to make a set of drums. Set the drums on baby's lap or between the two of you on the floor. Briefly demonstrate how to beat each drum with your fingers, palms, knuckles, and heels of the hand. Put some music on and tap to the beat.

Bowl or Pot Drums: Any bowl or pot can be turned upside down to make a drum. Set baby on a blanket on the floor surrounded by five or more different containers. Give her a wooden spoon or other objects for beating the drums. Sit down together with the many drums, turn on music, and drum along.

story sound effects

Ages: 12 months and up

Make up or read a familiar story to your child. The story should involve many sound effects, animals, and silly characters. As you tell the story, sing some of the words and have your child make all the sound effects.

Use any musical instruments you have to represent the appearance of one of the characters. For instance, when a fairy appears you might want to ring a bell, when the giant stomps in, try hitting a wooden block. Make up your own sound effects box to bring out whenever you tell a story.

★ **Wit & Wisdom** ★

It is easy to make your own sound effects. Use an old plastic film canister and fill it with various sound-making objects: dry beans, marbles, rice, popcorn, bells, or pebbles. I put one of the containers in my son's hand and let him shake it whenever I make a sound effect—he loves it!
—Deborah W., Fresno, California

funny song

153

Ages: 15 months and up

Singing is a good place for baby to start developing a sense of humor. Silly, ridiculous verses bring out giggles in baby even at one year old. Find some songs or make up one of your own. Start with everyday things like brushing teeth, and make them silly:

"This is the way we brush our toes. . . ."
"Twinkle, Twinkle, little donut . . . . "
"Mary had a little whale . . . . ."
"I know an old lady who swallowed a cow . . . ."
"Here we go over to grandmother's house . . ."

At the very least, you might laugh and baby might think—which promotes mental growth in both of you.

★ **Wit & Wisdom** ★

My daughter loves wacky, fun, nonsense songs. Her favorite singers are Linda Arnold, Joe Scruggs, and Raffi.
—Cindy A., West Bend, Wisconsin

louder, softer please

Ages: 15 months and up

Sing a familiar song, such as "Yankee Doodle." Start singing it loudly, gradually singing more softly, as if Yankee Doodle were riding off into the distance. Sing more of the song, this time getting louder and louder, as if Yankee Doodle were riding toward you.

This little exercise helps your child understand the dynamics of sound and music. Both of you can sing songs together, changing the volume to suit the words and meaning of the songs.

dramatic play

spider time

Ages: o and up

Cradle baby in your arms or lie next to baby on the floor. Use your hands and arms to act out this classic story about a tenacious little spider who just can't kick the water spout habit. One hand is the spider crawling upward, the other washes over it like rain. Circle your arms up around your sunny face. If holding baby, use your available hand to act out the spider's part.

The eensy, weensy spider
climbed up the water spout.
Down came the rain and
washed the spider out.
Out came the sun and
dried up all the rain.
So the eensy, weensy spider
climbed up the spout again.

(Traditional, Great Britain, North America)

horsey ride

Ages: 6 months and up

Materials
Several small bells
Ribbon or elastic

Sew or string bells onto the ribbon or elastic. Sit with baby in a rocker or comfortable chair and gently rock baby in your arms as you share this bouncing rhyme together.

Ride a cock horse to Banbury Cross
to see a fine lady (baby)
upon a white horse. (change color of horse to black, brown, gray, etc.)
With rings on her (his) fingers (jingle bells on baby's fingers)
and bells on her (his) toes (jingle bells on toes)
she (he) shall have music wherever she (he) goes.

(Traditional, Great Britain)

Bouncing on the knee is especially fun for older babies.

mr. moon

Ages: 6 months and up

Materials
Two paper plates
Watercolor markers
Straw or popsicle sticks
Tape

On one plate, draw the shape of a half-moon with a simple face, with eyes, nose, mouth, eyebrows, and chin. On the other plate, draw the shape of the sun with a face drawn on it too. One could be smiling, the other sad. Attach a straw or stick to the back of each with tape. Here is a sweet rhyme to say as you slowly and smoothly move the puppets for baby to watch. As the moon comes up the sun might go down and vice versa.

> *Mr. Moon, Mr. Moon*
> *You're up too soon.*
> *The Sun's still high in the sky.*
> *So go back to your bed,*
> *and cover up your head,*
> *and wait for the day to go by.*

About three weeks after birth, baby is able to distinguish between colors. Warm colors such as yellow, orange, and red are preferred to cool ones like blue and green. By eight weeks, baby begins to focus both eyes to make a single, somewhat blurred image. At approximately four months old, baby can focus and see clearly, and really see what you look like in those early morning hours!

ding-a-ling

Ages: 6 months and up

Materials
Toy telephone or real telephone no longer in use

Have a pretend conversation with someone special that baby knows, like grandma or grandpa. Talk about something you and baby did that day. Then give baby a turn. You can say, "Grandma wants to talk with you too." Listen to the sounds and intonations baby makes while on the phone. Does baby sound like someone you know? Exaggerate your vocal intonation and facial expressions while modeling phone communication skills. In no time baby will be trying to imitate your sounds.

★ Wit & Wisdom ★

Every week my mother, who lived out of state, would send my daughter a page cut out of a coloring book for her to color in and send back. This carried on until my daughter went to kindergarten and it formed a very special bond.
—Brooke M., Tuscon, Arizona

puppet play

Ages: 6 months and up

Puppets are usually baby's first experience with the idea of acting. It begins when mom or dad puts a puppet on a hand and talks to baby over the side of the crib, and from there the magic of imagination begins to bloom. Think of all the different scenarios that can be acted out with puppets. You can make paper three-inch tall shapes of baby's favorite characters and glue them to a popsicle stick to act out songs or stories when you sing or say them. When a toy is lost in the house you might get out the puppet who finds lost toys. As baby grows, the puppets can be used to act out feelings or different activities baby does during the day. Puppets also make a perfect travel toy, light and easy to carry.

when you do this, I do that

Ages: 9 months and up

Baby learns a lot about cause and effect through play. Ask baby to touch your nose. When he does, surprise him by sticking out your tongue. Do this a few times so baby expects you to stick your tongue out. Then surprise him again by doing something else when he touches your nose, like smiling, tickling him, or saying a funny word.

Next, fill your cheeks with air, then take baby's finger and push on your cheeks. As you let the air come out of your mouth your head tilts the right, as you fill your cheeks back up with air, your head sits straight on your shoulders again. Be creative and come up with other cause and effect games of your own.

simple costume design

Ages: 12 months and up

You don't need a sewing machine to be the world's best costume designer, at least in the eyes of your baby. Scraps of fabric, scarves, sheets, and pillowcases can be transformed into capes, princess skirts, and rivers for baby fish to swim in. The joy of childhood is that the costume doesn't have to look exactly like the wing of a bird or the top of a flower to become one. Open the pillowcase at the seams and cut a hole in the middle to make a cape, tie a few scarves around baby's waist to make a fairy skirt, wrap a piece of construction paper into the shape of a cone with a point and tape the scarf to the end of the hat to make a princess hat. Lay the scarves on the floor, taking one end to shake them as you pretend to be fish in a stream. Begin early on to make dramatic play part of your everyday interaction with baby.

a day at the races

Ages: 12 months and up

Materials
2 colored plastic straws
Cotton balls
Masking tape

Clear off the top of a table or lie down with baby on a rugless floor. Put a piece of tape down to mark the start and finish lines. Pretend that each of your cotton balls are horses, or race cars, or runners. Say, "On your mark, get set, go," then begin to blow at your cotton balls through the straw. In the beginning, both of you might want to blow at one cotton ball. Scream and cheer when the race is finished and the horse, car, or runner crosses the finish line.

★ Wit & Wisdom ★

I've started using a backpack instead of a diaper bag. It is much easier to carry around and leaves my hands free.
—Ben, Springfield, Illinois

set design

Ages: 12 months and up

An ordinary cardboard box is all you need to make the most elaborate set designs. Large appliance boxes make great playhouses, or can be opened up on one seam to form a standing screen of a castle, undersea world, spaceship, or zoo. If you want, paint the scenes you make and store them flat in the garage to be brought out with each new dramatic production.

★ Wit & Wisdom ★

My daughter is so excited when I get dressed up in funny clothes, whether it be a hat, a cape, or funny glasses. She gets really involved in the idea of putting things on and off my face.
—Brenda, Seattle, Washington

deep sea adventure

Ages: 12 months and up

Materials
Laundry basket or box large enough to sit in
Jump rope
Paper towel tube (use as spyglass and bullhorn)
Small blanket

Pretend to go on a deep sea adventure with baby. Use hands to paddle your boat, singing a boating song like, "Row, Row, Row Your Boat." Talk about creatures that live in the sea. Go for a swim (on the floor) kicking, paddling, and rolling around. Use your spyglass to search for land, and use the rope to tie up the boat. More props can be added, such as fish shapes cut from cardboard and colored with markers, or a child-size broom or plastic bat as an oar. The jump rope can be used for dramatic rescues with lots of pulling and tugging. Here's a rhyme to add spice to your adventure:

A sailor went to sea, sea, sea
To see what she could see, see, see
But all that she could see, see, see
Was the bottom of the deep blue sea, sea, sea.

what to become?

Ages: 15 months and up

Everyday outings are a great place to watch and learn what different people do, and how they act. Pull over the next time you see a construction site and watch what the construction workers do. A trip to a bakery, bank, pet store, or fire department might provide the perfect fuel for future dramatic games. The list of characters is endless: mail carrier, police officer, firefighter, grocery clerk, musician in band, farmer, orchestra conductor, truck driver, teacher, hairdresser, bus driver, train engineer, pilot, animal trainer, astronaut, circus performer, doctor, veterinarian, nurse, or dancer.

A simple prop or two helps baby to become the character. For example, if baby wants to play mail carrier and post office, use a shoe box for a mailbox, junk mail as "mail," and make a mailbag out of a brown paper bag (cut off the top and use it to make a shoulder strap), or canvas tote bag. Toy instruments, medical kits, tools, and dishes are great for enriching baby's play. A bike helmet can double as an astronaut's helmet or a construction worker's hard hat. A plastic bat, plastic golf club, or yardstick stuffed between some couch cushions could be the stick shift of a forklift, truck, or bus.

magic carpet ride

Ages: 15 months and up

Materials
Sheet, quilt, blanket, or large beach towel
Toys baby chooses

Take baby on a magic carpet ride. Have baby sit or lie on the blanket, say the magic words, and away you go. Then pull baby around, zigzagging as you go through the house. Say, "Wave to your friends." When your arms get tired of pulling baby, rest, and let baby take some of his toys for a ride. If the blanket seems too big for baby to pull, provide something more manageable. Some babies load up the blanket with as many toys as possible and then request another ride themselves! *Aladdin* is a good movie to watch to get baby thinking about magic carpets.

dress-up box

Ages: 15 months and up

Look through your closet for things you don't wear or want anymore: hats, gloves, slippers, shoes, belts, shirts, and pants. Find a big box and paint the outside or buy a special "dress-up" container. Put all your discarded items into the new dress up box. Let other people know you are looking for fun dress up clothes. Antique stores, thrift stores, and garage sales are good places to look. Keep your collection going and take time often to play dress-up with your baby. Make sure to hold baby in front of a mirror to see how both of you look. Baby will especially like seeing mom or dad in funny hats, dresses, or shoes. Take lots of pictures!

finder's keepers

Ages: 15 months and up

Materials
Clean box, large enough for baby to
  crawl into and play
Favorite toy, stuffed animal
Small blanket or beach towel
Flashlight

Tip box on its side and place favorite toy inside, then cover it with a blanket or towel. Say, "Let's hunt for your (name of toy). I don't see it anywhere, where is it?" Encourage baby to hold flashlight and lead the way. Narrate as you search using words that baby can attach to actions, such as behind, around, under, on top, over there, next to, near. Of course, you both know where the toy is. The box could be a cave, house, castle, or airplane. If space in the box permits, drape a towel over the opening and while baby is inside, peek your head in to make shadows on the side of the box with a flashlight. This game is especially fun if the room is dark.

nursery rhyme productions

Ages: 18 months and up

Nursery rhymes are fun to act out. They're short, usually silly or dramatic, and have characters baby has heard about. Here's one to try. Make up some of your own.

Jack and Jill Cooperate: Child-size step stool, small bucket or pail, torn pieces of newspaper or blue construction paper (for pretend water).

Jack and Jill went up the hill
to fetch a pail of water.
Jack fell down and broke his crown,
and Jill came tumbling after.
Jill and Jack went up the track
to fetch the pail again.
They climbed with care, got safely there,
and finished the job they began.

(From *Father Gander Nursery Rhymes* by Dr. Douglas W. Larche, Advocacy Press)

Pretend the stool is a hill. Hold baby's hand while baby steps up, then down, then tumble and roll on the floor together. Repeat it a second time, going over the stool, circling around with the bucket, and finishing the job together.

nature

backyard safety

Ages: o and up

Your own backyard, no matter how big, whether rural or city, will become baby's outdoor wonderland. Keep baby safe while she explores with the following tips:

- Be sure all pools, spas, and even a baby pool is surrounded by a fence of five feet or higher with a self-closing, self-latching gate. Make sure to empty baby pools when not in use.
- Be cautious with lawn mowers. Never take a child as a passenger on a ride-on lawn mower—he could slip and fall under the rotating blades that do not stop rotating for a few minutes after turning the engine off. Also, clear the area of rocks, sticks, or toys that might fly many feet in the air if struck by the mower and hit baby. Store all gas out of reach.
- Make sure decks, balconies, and gates are safe. Slats should be no more than three inches apart and the wood should be smooth with no exposed nails.
- Keep baby away from the barbecue at all times. Remember that it remains hot long after it is turned off. Also, check for any embers that might have blown from the grill.
- Check your plants. There are some common garden plants (castor bean, foxglove, oleander) that are poisonous. Don't let baby put any plant in her mouth; even if they aren't toxic, they do present a choking hazard.
- Be aware of neighborhood pets. Big dogs who run into your yard wagging their tails wanting to be friendly are terrifying to baby. Notify neighbors if you notice pets wandering into your yard.

meet the animals

Ages: 3 months and up

Even young babies are enchanted when in the presence of animals. Something about the color, sound, and movement puts them into a trance. If you don't have any animals of your own, consider a zoo or farm trip. Most zoos have a petting area, where baby can feed goats, lambs, horses, and sometimes a pig or two. Before you go to visit animals, look at picture books or watch a show about them. While at the zoo or farm, don't just stroll past. Instead, sit and watch your favorite animals for a little while, as it's the only way to get to know a particular animal's behavior.

★ Wit & Wisdom ★

When we eat our breakfast we look out the window trying to spot birds or squirrels. If we spot one we pretend we are both that animal eating our breakfast.
—Lauren Z., Atlanta, Georgia

feel the wind

Ages: 6 months and up

Take baby outside today to feel all kinds of new sensations. Things that are ordinary to you will be brand-new adventures for baby. If it's a warm summer day, feel the warmth of the sun. If there's a light rain, go out and feel the drops on your face. Let the wind blow through your hair, watch leaves float to the ground, or let snowflakes silently drift to the top of your tongue. Whatever the season, the outdoors offers endless possibilities. Smell a flower, walk barefoot through the grass, jump on a pile of leaves. Love of nature can be taught at a very young age and is communicated through a parent's enthusiasm, so enjoy your world!

sunrise

Ages: 6 months and up

Make a special plan to get up at sunrise (if you're not up already!). Plan to go outside and watch the sunrise together, then have a special breakfast. If you are up early nursing baby, take a sunrise walk. It is a special time of day, so quiet and fresh. Find a few children's poems or a Native American story about the sun and read it together. Remember, children learn to appreciate nature from their own experience of it.

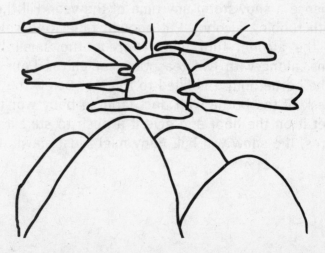

snowstorm

Ages: 6 months and up

Materials
Small plastic drink bottle with a lid
Rubbing alcohol
Blue food coloring
Small buttons, beads or sequins
Glitter
Clear vegetable oil

Experience a snowstorm any time of the year. Fill the plastic drink bottle with rubbing alcohol. Put enough blue food color in the bottle to make the alcohol turn blue. Drop in the small buttons, beads, or sequins, along with two teaspoons of glitter. Pour clear vegetable oil into the bottle until it is filled to the top. Screw the lid on tightly. Wrap the neck of the bottle with duct tape so baby won't be able to take it off. Set it on the floor and give it a push to start it rolling. As the bottle turns, the snow will fall. Baby might just crawl after it.

wish upon a star

Ages: 9 months and up

Materials
Books on stars
Glow-in-the-dark star stickers

Children are fascinated with stars. Read books about stars to baby, and teach her the song "Twinkle, Twinkle Little Star." Above the crib or bed, stick up glow-in-the-dark stars. Plan a night to take baby for a walk outside, point out stars, and make up stories about how stars have guided people to far-off places. Start the tradition of looking for a special star and making a wish on it.

what's that smell?

Ages: 12 months and up

Materials
Kitchen flavorings and spices
Foods that smell: salami, strawberries, yogurt, etc.
Perfumes, soaps, etc.
Flowers, grass, etc.

Make a game out of smelling the different flavorings, spices, foods, soaps, flowers, etc. around the house. As baby smells, tell him what he is smelling. If baby is old enough and already eating solid foods, let him taste the foods. It is fun to smell, and babies respond immediately to strong smells.

Take baby out of the kitchen and go from room to room finding things for baby to smell. Continue the fun outdoors with flowers, grass, dirt and anything else that might smell. As baby gets older, you might want to make a chart and put a happy or sad face next to the smells baby likes or doesn't like.

176

centerpiece

Ages: 12 months and up

When you go out for a walk today collect things like flowers, rocks, twigs, branches, bark, or feathers. When you get home, arrange all the things you found in some sort of vase-like container or box. Baby might just watch you, or she may help, but in any case she will be proud of her contribution when the family sits down to dinner. Put your display in the middle of the table where everyone eats. Tonight at dinner bring attention to the beautiful centerpiece, pointing out all the different things that were collected. Even a one-year-old will know she had something to do with the display, and feel proud to be part of it! Don't forget to take a photo to put into baby's artistic creations scrapbook!

sky's the limit

Ages: 12 months and up

Materials
Blanket
Stroller

Place baby on his back on top of the blanket. Lie down next to baby on the blanket and wonder together. Look up at the sky, notice the color, and look for clouds. Move the blanket under a tree and look up at the tree branches and leaves. Visually explore the sky and all you see in it. Make up stories about the clouds as they float by. Make up songs about the birds and butterflies. Relax and enjoy the peace together.

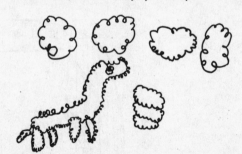

nature walk

Ages: 12 months and up

Materials
Large paper shopping bag
Items from nature
Scarf to use as a blindfold

Go outside together and gather nature's treasures: feathers, leaves, grass, stones, bark, flowers, and dirt. Put them in the large paper bag. When you have at least ten things in the bag, sit down with baby and play the following guessing game.

If baby wants to put the blindfold on do so, otherwise baby can close eyes and reach her hand into the bag to feel one item at a time. As she brings the item out of the bag you can describe what she is feeling. If baby has started talking, ask her to guess what the object is. After baby does this for a while, switch, and have the adult reach into the bag and guess.

bird watch

Ages: 15 months and up

- Make a bird feeder by rolling a pinecone first in peanut butter, then in the birdseed. Hang the bird feeder with string outside a window where it can be observed. Watch for birds to visit the feeder, and when they do, encourage baby to watch.
- Go to the library and check out a book on local birds. Look through the book and see if you can identify the birds at your feeder.
- Leave a basket full of colored yarn pieces outside. The birds in your yard just might steal the pieces and weave them into their nests. Walk around the yard and check for colorful nests.
- Buy a CD of bird sounds and listen to them. Next time you're outside baby might recognize the same sound and be thrilled to know it is a bird singing.

plant a seed

Ages: 15 months and up

Materials
Bean seed
Paper cup
Dirt

Plant the bean in a paper cup. Help baby to water the seed when needed. Children are excited when something actually grows! Remember, even before children talk, they observe. Make sure they know the growing plant belongs to them, and point it out to other family members as well. Older babies might want to decorate the cup first or go to the store and get a cheap clay pot to decorate with markers, crayons, and paint.

shadow play

Ages: 15 months and up

Once you introduce baby to his shadow, there are many games to play.

- Do simple movements and watch how your shadows move, point out baby's shadow at different times of the day, try to make the shadows grow bigger or smaller.
- Stand in place on a hard surface, like a driveway or deck, and have baby decorate your shadow with leaves. Then have baby stand and you decorate his shadow (quickly!).
- Play shadow tag. Instead of tagging baby, all you have to do is tag his shadow.
- Take a towel or sheet, moving it from side to side so that baby's shadow changes when just an arm, leg, or head might be sticking out.

special tree

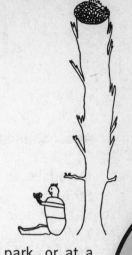

Ages: 15 months and up

Materials
Buy a seedling tree
Small shovel

Find a place to plant your tree; in your yard, at a local park, or at a nearby school. On baby's birthday—or any special day you choose—go with baby to plant the tree. Once the tree is planted, go back often to water and care for it. Tell baby the tree belongs to her and do the following things together: watch the tree grow and change, measure baby and measure the tree, name the tree, care for the tree, play and sing around baby's tree. Talk about how trees grow, get a picture book from the library so baby can see what the inside of a tree looks like. Take pictures of baby standing next to the tree every six months—have a contest to see who is growing faster—baby or tree.

★ **Wit & Wisdom** ★
A young tree is a great gift to send a parent or grandparent when a new baby is born. This is a constant reminder to the receiver of their very special child.
—Shirley C., Lockford, California

183

let's go fishing

Ages: 18 months and up

Materials
String
Stick or pole
Kitchen magnet
Steel paper clips
Wading pool
Colorful sponges

Tie the string to the stick or pole. Attach a kitchen magnet to the end of the string. Cut the sponges into fish shapes. Push the steel paper clips into the sponge. Throw the fish into the wading pool, or onto the ground if no pool is available. Cast your string into the pool and get your camera ready for baby to hook his catch.

leaf masks

Ages: 18 months and up

Materials
Paper plate
Yarn or ½-inch wide elastic
Clear tape

Cut the paper plate in half. Hold the paper plate up to baby's face. Mark a place for his eyes and nose. Cut a triangle where his nose is so the point of the triangle rests on the top of his nose and the bottom of the triangle is open; this will make the mask more comfortable to wear. Cut out the eye holes. Punch holes on either side of the mask and tie a yarn strap through each one, or use one piece of elastic tied from side to side. Using the clear tape, help baby to tape the leaves onto the mask one row at a time, covering the tape as you go.

★ Wit & Wisdom ★

The first time I put on a mask to play with my son, he started to cry. Then I figured out that I needed to put on the mask while he was watching so he understood that my face was underneath.
—David, Oklahoma City, Oklahoma

storytelling

read from the beginning

Ages: 6 months and up

Baby learns to read by being surrounded by language, seeing others read, and being read to. At first, baby will lie or sit on your lap, enjoying the closeness and sounds of your voice. Then baby will become actively interested in the books themselves: touching, smelling, and tasting, as well as looking at them. Baby may hit the pages in excitement, then point at pictures, turn the pages, and eventually babble about the pictures. Let baby "read" you her favorite story. Your attention and enthusiasm will make reading and sharing books so rewarding for baby she will learn to truly love books!

stuffed friends

Ages: 6 months and up

Babies have a knack for attracting large quantities of stuffed animals, dolls, and creatures of unknown origin. Put them to use by casting them in stories you tell. They don't have to be a puppet to be used like one. If you happen to have toys that are similar, such as two teddy bears, bunnies, or kittens, then you have a family, so to speak. Some themes are more popular than others, depending on baby's personality and stage of development. Favorites may include getting lost, then found, going on a journey, driving different vehicles, climbing hills to find something, looking for mother, going to the zoo, birthday parties, and being in a parade. Take your cue from baby.

★ Wit & Wisdom ★

When too many stuffed animals take over baby's room...pick out a few to donate to children in need, the Salvation Army, local churches or shelters. Starting this early in baby's life will teach him a lot about giving.
—Lauren Z., Atlanta, Georgia

do i have one for you

Ages: 9 months and up

We all have stories to tell and they come from various sources. Some can be found in our dreams, some from our memory, some from people we've known or books we've read. A few we simply imagine! Well, there's no time like the present to relax, clear your head of the day's events, and think about your life experiences, people, pets, places lived, fears, favorite things, wishes you had or have, or family traditions.

As you take this journey into your memory, bring back something to share with baby. Tell it as you remember, or change it to what you want to communicate today. Even though baby might not understand all of what you say, he hears your passion for the telling and enjoys and is comforted by your voice. You create the story. Stories grow and change over time with the telling. Much can be learned about yourself, and at the same time, baby is learning to love language and the art of story-telling.

remember what we did today?

Ages: 12 months and up

Even if baby may not be speaking, parents can begin to teach their children early about beginnings, middles, and ends of stories by taking the time each day to go over daily events, excursions, and experiences. Let's say you went to the park that day. Begin at the beginning, and give baby a few details, following chronologically that specific event. "We got to the park and saw the white dog, then we played in the sand, went down the slide, ate lunch, and swung." Give baby a chance to fill in some of the words. This teaches baby how to remember life events in story form.

draw and tell

Ages: 12 months and up

Materials
Piece of white paper
Crayons

Think of a short, simple story either made up or from a book. Get out the piece of paper, and as you tell it from memory, draw the story. Simple stick figures or scribbles will do. As you draw things mentioned in the story, a scene will take shape in picture form. Color things in as you go. Baby will be enchanted with the way shapes take form as you talk. Make up a story about baby—he will love a story about himself.

As baby gets older, let him tell you a story as you draw quickly what you are hearing. This form of drawing is more like a diagrammed progression of the story, told with lines, shapes, and stick figures, rather than a piece of art with everything colored in. So, don't be shy give it a try even if you can't draw!

auditioning all dolls

Ages: 12 months and up

Encourage pretend play with dolls. Dolls are fun because they look like real people so baby might easily relate to and dramatize the everyday things a doll might do. Have baby feed doll or pretend with it. Identify body parts on characters and begin to act out scenarios. Ask baby to act out a story as you are reading it to them. Or you each take one doll and after you read part of a picture book, act out the story with the dolls. Paper dolls are also fun to make. Use a sturdy piece of cardboard and cut out the basic shape of a doll. Help baby to color in clothes on doll to match the character in a favorite book.

★ **Wit & Wisdom** ★

Whenever my daughter was given a new doll, we would make up a story about where she came from, what her name was, what she liked to do. I wrote them all down in a special doll book.
—Jane, Hollywood, Florida

little performer

Ages: 12 months and up

Babies love to hear their voices over a microphone. Buy a toy microphone or echo microphone. Begin by making a nonsense sound into the microphone, like Baaa, Daaa, Maaa. Now put the microphone in front of baby's mouth. As imitative skills increase, you can elongate the complexity of the sounds. This is a fun way to strengthen muscles needed for speaking; it also encourages baby to enjoy all the different sounds she can make. As baby gets older, she may begin to recite nursery rhymes or familiar songs. Make sure you announce the performer with "Ladies and Gentlemen, Boys and Girls . . . Introducing Melissa Lynn on the microphone." Followed by applause, of course.

baby's day book

Ages: 12 months and up

Take photos of baby throughout one day. Make sure to include pictures of his room, toys, brothers or sisters, mom or dad, the family pet, backyard, stroller, and a meal or two. Put the pictures in chronological order in a picture book. Encourage baby to turn the pages and tell you the story. This book will be helpful for baby when he starts at a day care center. You can bring the book with him in his backpack. Teachers can learn about the family, baby's likes and dislikes, favorite characters, and toys. You might also want to take similar pictures of baby's day while at day care and put those into a book for baby to bring home.

baby's adventure

Ages: 18 months and up

Go on an outing with baby: a walk around the block, a trip to the pet store, a visit to a neighbor, out to pick flowers, or anything else that interests both of you. Make sure as you walk to point out interesting things along the way. When you get home, get out a large piece of paper or open flat a paper grocery bag, and begin drawing. Make a picture map, telling baby as you draw what you did together. Start at your front door and draw everything from that point until you returned home. Use simple stick drawings or scribbles if need be. As baby gets older, she can tell you what she did and you can draw it. Later, baby can draw as well. Remember, her drawing may not resemble anything. However, she might put down a scribble, and know exactly what it is! Let her tell you what she sees—it will be fun for both of you!

rotating picture tale

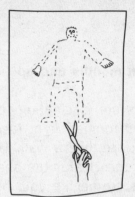

Ages: 18 months and up

Materials
Old magazine
Scissors
Glue
Piece of Paper

Look through magazines together. If baby points to a picture, or seems interested, cut it out. Glue the pictures onto the white paper. Put one picture onto each sheet. Once all the pictures are glued on, make up a story about them. Change the story a few times by shuffling the pictures, starting with a different picture, then adding the others to the story's plot. Since baby picked the pictures, she will feel a great sense of involvement and pride in her homemade story.

shadow blasters

Ages: 18 months and up

Shadows are fascinating to watch and fun to form. All you need is a darkened room, a light (even a flashlight will do), and a flat, light colored surface, like a wall. The stronger the light and the whiter the flat surface, the clearer the shadow picture will be. Change the size of the shadows by moving your hands closer to the light or farther away. One of the simplest shadows to cast is a rabbit. You do this by holding two fingers up in a peace sign. Experiment using one hand. Then use one hand, with the other hand over the top or underneath. Experiment further by adding features to animals, like a snail, turtle, dog, goose, moose, alligator, crab, and bird. Make up your own stories and rhymes to go with shadows you create: "There was a tiny snail that moved so slow, she came out when it rained to stretch and grow, she nibbled on leaves and all the yellow flowers, even though it rained and rained for hours." Have fun with words and you'll surprise yourself!

on the go

where to go

Ages: o and up

Here is a list of fun places to go with baby. If you are not sure what is available in your area, look for a local parenting paper. Many community recreation centers may also be able to help. The local library is also a great source for finding out about things.

Children's concerts or plays
Fairs, exhibitions, or
   theme parks
Children's museums
Zoo or farm
Fire station
Police station
Local stores
Bakery, dairy

Flower shows
Boating shows
Home shows
Major sporting events
Circus
Ice shows
Parks
Art museums
Television station

The list is endless. Remember, everything is new to baby, so point out things to him that you find interesting. Take baby places where he can get a hands-on experience. If you are at a performance of some sort, make sure to sit near an exit, as baby may get bored halfway through. Make sure to pack treats. Good luck!

travel tips

The key to successful traveling with a baby is preparation and a good sense of humor.

- Make a list of everything you need for your baby before leaving: baby toiletries, first-aid kit, Benadryl, a thermometer, plastic bags of all sizes, and other supplies you think might be useful.
- Pack on-the-go baby-proofing supplies like socket protectors, masking or duct tape to attach electric cords to the wall, a toilet lock, and rubber bands to keep baby out of cabinets.
- Pack books and toys to keep him entertained in the car, plane, or hotel room. Many games can be played with a few supplies: a flashlight, old sheet, and few puppets are light and pack flat. Flashlight can be used for flashlight tag, going on safari in a dark room to find toys, or shining around the room to identify objects. A sheet becomes a fort, river, or cape, and kids can either roll up in them or they can be unrolled and used to give "magic carpet rides."
- Don't forget a bag of wrapped-up treats for your baby to pick from a few times an hour.

car games

Ages: 3 months and up

- Go through magazines, old picture books, or the family picture album and pick out pictures that baby especially likes. Take them to a copy store and have the pictures laminated. Punch a hole through them, run a piece of twine through them and pin them to the seat with a large safety pin.

- Make a cassette tape including family voices, read a story, sing a song, or simply talk into the tape. Play this tape in the car and watch as baby tries to figure out how this mystery of sound is happening when nobody's mouth is moving!

- Make colored spyglasses using cardboard toilet paper tubes, different colors of cellophane, rubber bands, and yarn or string. Cut the cellophane into four- to five-inch squares. Wrap cellophane over the end of one of the tubes and secure it with a rubber band. Make many of these tubes of different colors, and string them together to hang in the car, ready for baby to look out the window.

- Make an edible necklace using Cheerios or Fruit Loops and a thin shoelace with plastic tips. String Cheerios onto the shoestring and tie both ends together making a necklace. When baby is hungry he can eat part of the necklace. Wash the shoelaces afterwards and use them again.

restaurant tips

If you're going to a restaurant with baby, remember:

- Go when the restaurant is not busy.
- Make sure that baby is hungry.
- If food is taking too long tell your server you will be outside playing with your child, and ask if he could call you when the food arrives.
- Get crackers or bread and ask if they have crayons and paper.
- Pick restaurants that are set up for children with kid's menus and high chairs.
- As soon as the child gets restless, order dessert or ice cream.
- You will probably not get dessert or coffee yourself, so save that for a time you're out without baby.
- Praise baby for all good behavior!

restaurant games

Hide a Hand: Hide something in one hand and then close your fists. Show baby both fists and have her guess where the prize is. Make up a pattern so baby can begin to predict where the prize will be.

Hide-and-Seek: Hide a coin, sugar packet, a key, or some other small item somewhere on the table while the other player has her eyes closed. Open eyes and try to spot object.

Count Together: Kids love to count anything and everything. They will soon get used to counting from one to ten if you do it often enough. You can count all sorts of things in the restaurant or on your table.

Drawing Games: Carry masking tape and crayons in your purse so you're always prepared to tape down the free paper place mats. Baby loves to scribble but may not be coordinated enough yet to hold the paper down while he draws.

★ Wit & Wisdom ★

When I carry my daughter in her car seat, I found the plastic handle would dig into my hand. I decided to cushion it with tennis-racket grip tape and now I don't mind carrying her.
—Amanda L., Beaver Dam, Wisconsin

napkin art

Materials
Paper napkins
Scissors

Make a point of carrying around a pair of small scissors in your purse or in baby's bag. While sitting and waiting at a restaurant, pull the scissors out and make fascinating works of art out of napkins. Baby will be mesmerized watching you snip away, then reveal a beautiful snowflake or people chain. Here's how you do it:

Snowflake: Fold napkin in half two times. Cut triangular and circular notches out of the edges all along the square. Fold the square in half and cut a few notches in the middle. Try this once and you'll see you can basically cut anywhere and a beautiful snowflake will still emerge. Open up the square and see what you get.

People Chain: Open napkin up, then fold napkin at least three times in the same direction. Draw half a person, making sure to have the arm go out to the joined edge. Cut around the drawing and open it up, and you will have a chain of people holding hands.

finding a lost child

Precautions to take so you don't lose your child:

- Dress child in bright, easy-to-spot clothing.
- Keep a recent color photograph in your wallet.
- Make sure your child has identification. Write down your personal information as well as the hotel (if on vacation) and put it in her pocket or in her shoe tag.
- Carry a detailed written description of your child, including height, weight, hair and eye color, birthmarks, pierced ears, etc. Make sure to update it every few months.
- If you are with another adult, communicate clearly who is to be watching the baby. Switch off being responsible so that each adult can have a rest and enjoy the outing.
- If child is more than one year old, tell them before arriving at a public place that if they get lost to stand still and wait for you to find them.

What to do if you do:

- Calm down. Overreacting will slow the search.
- Secure other kids: If you have other kids with you, find someone to watch them.
- Use your voice and call out your baby's name. They may not see you but they might hear you.
- Get help immediately: stores, amusement parks, and other public places have procedures in place for finding children. The more people looking, the better.
- If there's a public address system, use it. Give a first name and description of your child.
- Give a detailed description of what your child was wearing, a physical description, as well as any insights as to things your child might be drawn to.
- Call the police if your child isn't found within several minutes, give them your location, and ask that they come and help you.

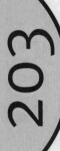

grocery store game

Take baby to the grocery store to explore, not to buy. Put baby in a shopping cart as you talk about how exciting the store is. Tell her about all the new things she will see and feel. Start wheeling the grocery cart up and down the aisles. If you see baby looking at, or reaching for something, hand it to her as you continue to hold the item with them. Rub the container against baby's hand, talk about the following things: shape, color, what is in it, whether it feels cold or hot, or rough or smooth. If you plan on buying anything it might be fun to taste test as well. Go through the store, letting baby investigate everything until baby loses interest.

★ Wit & Wisdom ★

If baby has become attached to some sort of blanket, cut a piece of it off to take on trips, instead of dragging the whole thing everywhere you go.
—Peter W., Carson City, Nevada

shopping cart safety

Many children are admitted to emergency rooms every year as a result of shopping cart injuries.

- Avoid putting baby in lightweight carts that have narrow wheels. All baby has to do is reach for something and the cart is likely to tip over.
- Use a seat belt. Most carts are not equipped with safety belts, but harness-type safety belts can be purchased and kept in the car for times you take baby shopping.
- Never attach your own car seat to the cart, the extra weight might make the cart unsteady. You can put the car seat in the bigger basket.
- Don't allow baby to push the cart around for fun, and don't allow siblings to push baby around while you shop.
- Never put baby in the big basket—even if it seems like more fun for baby to be able to sit and play while you shop.

Note:
A baby's memory is active from the very beginning, so don't miss opportunities for baby to soak in information. Place baby's stroller facing children at play while in the park, take baby to everyday places like the grocery store, and make sure baby has a clear view of family dinners.

silly photo

Materials
Find an instant photo booth

Think of some silly pictures you can take with baby, for example: kiss nose, chew finger, touch cheeks, or make silly faces. Put your change into the photo booth and create those silly pictures. Show them to your baby when they are finished, and when you get home hang them up somewhere baby can see them often. Talk about them once in awhile, telling baby how much fun you have when you are together, and how much you love him.

★ Wit & Wisdom ★

On a trip to the mall, I discovered that my fifteen-month-old son loved to drag things behind him. He was crying to be picked up as we walked the long trek to the parking lot. I had packages in my hands, so I decided to take off my belt and let him drag it. He then walked willingly to the car.
—Jessica B., Columbia, Maryland

i spy

Ages: 12 months and up

This might be a game you remember playing when you were a child. The object is to give baby word clues, using words in baby's vocabulary, then have baby guess what the object is. "I spy with my little eye something that is big, has a lot of hair, and barks when someone comes to the door." "I spy with my little eye something that is yellow, has a peel, monkeys eat them, and they taste sweet." The possibilities are endless. Add or subtract clues based on child's response. This is fun to play anyplace. Let older brothers and sisters participate in making up clues.

★ Wit & Wisdom ★

I found a way to save my car upholstery from dirty little hands. I put a crib sheet over the backseat. It fits perfectly, comes off easily and can be thrown into the washing machine at the end of the day.
—Barb B., Waialua, Hawaii

travel kit for fun

Materials
Flashlight
Puppets
Old scarves
Scissors
Masking tape
Bubbles
Paper grocery bags
Crayons

All of the above supplies will fit into a small shoe box. Put the flat grocery bags at the bottom of your suitcase if you don't want to fold them up. With these basic light and compact supplies you can play at least ten games.

- **Flashlight:** tag, shadow play, light race (have person shine the light and kids race to the light).
- **Puppets:** put on dramatic shows.
- **Old scarves:** Dress-up play, tape scarves to furniture to become forts, scarf shuffle.
- **Scissors:** Make masks out of the paper bags, napkin art.
- **Bubbles:** catch the bubble.
- **Paper bags:** open up to use as drawing paper, make a trip story, tape together to draw a scene for puppet show, do bag skits (put random items from around the room into the bag and have adult or kids make up a funny skit using everything that is in the bag).

picking a vacation location

Depending on your sense of adventure, a vacation can be as simple or as exotic as you desire. Having a baby does not mean you are limited in your travel choices, it just means that you will have to prepare differently for your trips.

- First, select a family-friendly destination. Make sure there are enough attractions (zoos, museums, parks, theaters, and playgrounds) to keep your trip interesting while having a comfortable place to relax and rest in.
- Second, find lodging that is baby-friendly. An upscale hotel or small bed and breakfast may not prove hospitable to baby's nighttime wailing or tantrums in the lobby.
- Third, select a destination that you truly want to visit. If you make concessions in your travel choice for the baby, you are setting yourself up for a tiresome and miserable vacation.
- Don't forget the option of planning a vacation at home. Take your phone off the hook, order take-out food, go to local baby-friendly attractions, or hire a baby-sitter while you go to an adult event and leave baby happily at home.
- Finally, remember that a vacation is supposed to be relaxing. Take things slowly, enjoy your baby, and relax.

child care/
playgroups

playing the day care game

There are many forms of day care available. Figuring out what type of care is right for your baby is the first step.

Center Care: Is run out of a child care center of some sort. High number of children, usually the kids are grouped together by age. May have many different caregivers. Positives: located near work location so might be able to visit at lunch, exposed to lots of other kids, many caregivers so one will usually click with child's personality.

Family Care: Is usually run out of someone's home, often located in a local neighborhood. Usually attended by a small amount of children of various ages. Usually one consistent caregiver. Positives: lower turnover rate of caregivers, kids exposed to less germs, often located near family home.

Nanny Care: A nanny is someone who lives in your home or comes to your home daily to care for your children. Sometimes two or more families will share one nanny, who will care for all the children in one of the families' homes. Nannies often do other forms of housework, like cooking, shopping, cleaning, or laundry. Positives: your child doesn't need to be driven to child care, no problem if child is sick.

day care checklist

When picking a day care you might have many questions. Don't feel silly asking them! You have a right to find out exactly how your baby will be treated.

- Will your baby be safe, well fed, comfortable, and valued?
- How do the caregivers respond to baby? Do the parenting styles match yours?
- Do caregivers express affection and have playful attitudes?
- Find out what the turnover rate is. Will your baby have to get to know many caregivers over a year's time, or does the center assign one primary caregiver to each baby?
- Are parents allowed to visit during the day to nurse or play? If so, proximity to work or home is important.
- Does the center rotate toys so that baby is exposed to new activities? Is the environment engaging? What kinds of activities will baby be exposed to?
- Is the staff or provider open to talking with parents who have developmental, behavioral, or other questions?
- Is the center or family child care provider licensed? What are the credentials of the caregiver or center staff?
- Does the staff have CPR and first-aid training?
- Have caregivers had a police check to determine whether they have a criminal record?

Note: Resource and referral agencies that provide lists of licensed child care facilities: Child Care Aware (800-424-2246), National Association for the Education of Young Children (800-424-2460), National Association for Family Child Care (800-359-3817).

hiring a baby-sitter

Here are some things to think about when hiring a baby-sitter:

- The first thing to think about is what you need most: someone to do the housework so you can be with baby, or someone to take care of baby?
- Make a list of what the job entails: baby-sitting, laundry, cooking, shopping, or housework.
- Word-of-mouth recommendations are best, but at any rate check references. Putting an ad in the paper outlining job expectations is another possible source.
- Once the applicant is in front of you, explain all the things on your list that you would expect her to do. There is nothing worse than hiring someone who doesn't really want to do the job.
- Check if sitter has had first-aid and CPR classes. Make sure to leave emergency numbers as well as where you can be reached in an emergency.
- Since baby can't talk, have the sitter keep a journal of the day's events: how long baby napped, when he went to the bathroom, what he ate, if they went for a walk, and what baby played with. If you want to make it easier, just make a worksheet and let them fill in the blanks.
- If you have doubts about the sitter's competence, have a friend or neighbor drop by unexpectedly to see how things are going. Or leave a tape recorder on to see how the baby is being treated. It is your right as a parent to expect good caregiving.

baby-sitter training

It is always a good idea to invite a prospective new baby-sitter over for a training session before you leave your baby with the sitter for the first time. Many parents make the mistake of assuming that a sitter has experience in every area of child rearing and that he knows exactly what you expect. Here are some things you'll want to go over.

- Discipline guidelines. Don't just tell him what your discipline guidelines are, role-play what you mean so he is clear on how you would like him to act.
- Show him where everything is that he might need. Emergency phone numbers, first-aid information, the kids' favorite toys, diapers, food, where the dog stays—whatever you think is important to make him comfortable with the running of your home.
- Provide a list of food restrictions as well as a list of all the things your baby can eat.
- If you expect him to do any cleaning up when you are gone, tell him what you expect. You may ask that he put the kids' toys away and clean up the kitchen, or you might want him to spend all his time attending baby. Just be clear.
- Play the "what-if" game with him. Give him different scenarios and ask him what he would do if that situation happened. Assure him that you are not judging him by his wrong answers, but rather want to make sure he is prepared.

organizing a playgroup

A playgroup is usually three children per one adult. It can be a group of children each with their parent, or one parent watching three children. The idea of the group is to let babies interact with each other, thereby learning beginning social skills. If you and your child could benefit from interacting with other babies and mothers, here are some ideas on how to get a playgroup started.

- Ask your friends if they want to set a weekly date to get babies together.
- Make sure one parent isn't always doing the "baby-sitting." If so, he or she should be paid.
- If you don't have friends with small children, go to a local park and look for other children close in age. Other places to look are day care centers, church, or put an add in the local paper. Mothers' clubs or groups are also a good place to go.
- Once you have a few people interested, get together and talk about parenting philosophies to make sure you feel comfortable with each other.
- Plan one month's worth of play dates, then give it a try.
- Talk together for ten minutes after each playgroup about how the interaction went, what the children liked and disliked, and brainstorm activities for the next gathering.

playgroup leaders' responsibilities

- There should be no more than three children to one adult.
- Babies and toddlers are completely dependent on adults to meet their needs, so must always be supervised.
- Talk to children one-to-one. Let children initiate conversation, then respond to them. If they don't talk yet, speak to them describing what's going on around them.
- Be supportive of skills they are trying. Praise children often.
- Respond promptly to crying.
- Respect a child's desire to carry around a favorite object.
- If children fight over a toy, an adult should step in, offering a like toy so each child may have one.
- Try to limit use of the word "no" to safety issues.
- Greet each child with a warm smile.
- Model for children how to use words instead of being aggressive, e.g., "I want to go on the swing" instead of pushing the other child off.
- Have an appropriate play area set up with activities planned.
- Set up a predictable routine to be followed each time.
- Provide healthful snacks frequently, especially liquids.

parent questionnaire

Make up a questionnaire for parents to fill out. Put this questionnaire in a folder that goes to the house where the playgroup is being held. Here are a few things the questionnaire should include:

- Emergency phone numbers: doctor, work number, alternate person to call for help.
- Food: likes, dislikes, and feeding schedule.
- Daily schedule with preferred nap times.
- Favorite toys or blanket.
- Favorite song.
- How to calm baby when crying.
- If baby is afraid of anything around the house (cat, dog).
- Names of brothers and sisters.

Put anything on the questionnaire that might make the relationship between the playgroup leader and child more supportive of the child's needs. Make sure this folder is wherever the babies are. Good luck!

NAME_____
ADDRESS_____
PHONE_____

NAP TIME_____

LIKES_____
_____
_____
_____

DISLIKES_____
_____
_____
_____

calm down

Materials
Soft rubber ball or beach ball

A great way to relax children after active play is a ball massage. Have all the children lie on a carpeted floor or soft mattress. Gently roll the ball, starting at their toes and rolling up to their chins. Then do each arm and leg separately. Do one child, then move on to the next. Babies will most likely giggle with anticipation of their upcoming turn. Say, "Ball is rolling, rolling, rolling, it's going to get you!"

group songs with actions

Little Rabbit Foo Foo

This old song is a favorite of young children who love to see the stuffed rabbit hopping around and getting scolded for bad behavior. They will giggle throughout and thoroughly enjoy waving their own fingers at the rabbit.

Little Rabbit Foo Foo, (stuffed rabbit hops around)
Hopping through the forest,
Scooping up the field mice, (rabbit pretends to scoop up a mouse)
And bopping them on the head. (rabbit bops mouse lightly on the head)
Down came the Good Fairy, (sprinkle hands down from above your head)
And she said: "Little Rabbit Foo Foo,
I don't want to see you (shaking index finger, indicating no in front of stuffed rabbit's nose)
Scooping up the field mice, (fairy scoops up field mice)
and bopping them on the head.
I'll give you two (or however many you want)
more chances, (hold up number of fingers)
And if YOU misbehave, (all the kids wag their fingers)
I'll turn you into a frog.

Hokey Pokey

Stand in a circle and follow what the song says.

You put your left hand in
You put your left hand out
You put your left hand in
and shake it all about
You do the Hokey Pokey and
You turn yourself around
That's what it's all about. Hey!

The verses continue with right hand, left foot, right foot, head, stomach, whole body, etc.

circle time

Circle time is when all the children sit in a circle, tell stories, share something, play games, sing songs, and enjoy being in a group. Circle time is especially fun when there is a parent for each child. Read a few stories and ask the children about the characters as you read, or say things not in the book, like "Do you see the red cape? Where is it?" Children love animation, so be expressive with your voice. Then let the children share something they might have brought with them. If they are too young to share something, hold up something they brought and tell everyone what it is. It's fun to sing a few songs together, or dance to some music. Finger puppets are also nice to tell stories with. If the kids are old enough, have them put together a small puppet show to perform. Circle time activities are endless. Remember not to make the children sit still for too long, as their attention spans are very short!

obstacle course

Every baby loves scooting around, crawling through tunnels, bouncing balls, and jumping up and down. Make simple obstacle courses for the children to go through. Include things like running to the tree, then hopping to the rock, crawling to the flower, then clapping two times. After all the children have done one obstacle course a few times, change it around and do it again. Babies will giggle as they watch each other crawling about. Try doing the course playing "follow the leader," with the leader making up what comes next.

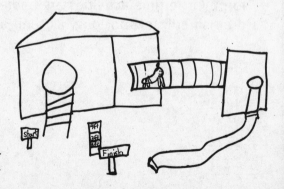

★ Wit & Wisdom ★

I found a fast way to get my daughter's shoes on when I was in a hurry to go out. Instead of wrestling with her on the floor trying to get her to hold her feet still, I put her in her high chair, gave her something to munch on and tied her shoes in peace.
—Mandy B., Toledo, Ohio

220

common games

Here are some games you probably played in your childhood but may have forgotten.

Simon Says: This is a simple copycat game. Start by saying "Simon says touch your toes," and demonstrate touching your toes. Your child then copies you. Repeat with simple gestures. Then let the child be the leader. You can use your own names instead of Simon.

Hide-and-Seek: With young children, play hide-and-seek in a small space so you know where everyone is. Small children don't always get the concept that you shouldn't see them. They will be hiding out in the open, or curling up in a ball pretending not to be seen. Play along and say, "Where is (child's name)?" even if you can see them.

Follow the Leader: One person leads, usually in a walking line. Everyone has to do what the leader does, and go wherever he or she goes.

Think of any other games you used to play, or better yet, ask your parents and see what they can remember!

co-op baby-sitting

Co-op baby-sitting is different from a playgroup. A co-op is arranged as a baby-sitting option. It takes some organization, but can be very effective and successful. This is how it works. There is a list of people who belong to the co-op. When you need a baby-sitter, you can call the co-op list of names until you find someone who is available. There is a person who keeps track of everyone's hours. If you baby-sit three hours, then the co-op owes you three hours, so you don't exactly pay the person back who baby-sat for you. Co-op baby-sitting is generally done in the home of the person doing the baby-sitting, since most people involved also have children. The co-op can be as big or small as you like. It's a good opportunity to meet other parents and save money on baby-sitting at the same time. Take some time to brainstorm ways you could organize a co-op so you could have a little time to yourself.

saying good-bye

No good-bye is said without some feeling! Tears don't make it a bad good-bye, after all, many adults cry in airports. Here are some ways to help good-byes go smoother.

1. Realize your child may react in a variety of ways: crying, sulking, thumb-sucking, or defying adult requests. This behavior is normal.
2. A gradual separation is best for young children. Leave them for a short amount of time, gradually working up to the full amount of time you intend to be away.
3. The child needs to feel safe in the new environment, so stay around a while to explore together.
4. Let your child tell you how they feel. Listen and say back to her what you have heard. Then tell her you will miss her too, but will be back.
5. Leave something with your child that reminds them of you: a scarf, a set of house keys, a glove, or an audiotape of your voice.
6. Be honest. Don't say you'll be right back if you won't.
7. NEVER sneak out!

★ Wit & Wisdom ★

To ease the transition from my being home to day care, I used day care for a few hours a day the week before I had to return to work. It gave my son time to get to know his caregiver, and gave us time to get used to the new routines.
—Jill B., Ventura, California

parks, playgrounds, and outdoor play

be prepared

Ages: 0 and up

Make a park kit to keep in your house or car that is full of special, practical things that will make your trips to the park more carefree and fun. Purchase or find a large canvas tote or a shopping bag with handles. Fill it with things that are "must-haves" on almost all outings to the park:

- Blanket or large beach towel
- First-aid kit
- Sunscreen
- A few paper bags for collecting things
- Sand toys, such as a pail, shovel, funnel, sifter, vehicles, and small toy animals
- Extra diapers and wipes
- Umbrella for rain or shine
- Magnifying glass for investigating

Add to this list as you discover what your park needs are. Having a kit like this makes going to the park much easier to prepare for.

a place to park

Ages: 6 months and up

Stop by your city parks and recreation department and ask if they have a park directory. If not, go exploring on your own. Keep a small notebook describing the facility for future reference. Make sure to keep maps or directions to the park in case a baby-sitter will be taking baby to the park. You will soon discover all parks are not the same. Some are older, with metal play structures in need of repair, while others contain brand-new equipment. Some have baby swings and areas specially designed for babies and small children, while others are geared more for the school-age child. Things to consider when checking out a park:

- Do you feel safe there?
- Are there bathrooms?
- Are there working water fountains?
- Is the park kept clean?
- Is there shade for sunny days?
- What types of activities is the park used for?
- Are pets allowed?
- What is the age range for the play equipment—will there be something for baby to play on?

anticipate problems

Curiosity and determination can land baby in situations that are more challenging than baby is physically ready for. Always be alert and anticipate situations where baby may need your help or words of warning. Areas to watch closely are:

- Swings: they don't have brakes and children using them are not always watching for curious babies.
- Don't assume older children at the park will be careful around baby. Many don't even notice and are simply not aware.
- If the park is busy, remove baby from the bottom of the slide so the next child's feet don't end up in baby's back.
- Babies love merry-go-rounds, both to ride on and to watch. They will not wait for it to stop before trying to hitch a ride, so you must be close enough to hold baby back. Be sure to warn them of the danger.

Accidents do happen, but fewer happen when baby is carefully supervised.

swing rhythm

Ages: 3 months and up

Some babies could swing the whole day through. Until baby is able to hold up his head, swing together gently on the big swings. When baby's neck and head are strong enough, introduce the baby swing. A rolled up baby blanket makes a nice cushion around baby and fills in some of the extra space inside the baby swing. Push baby gently from the front so you can look at each other—you'll know when baby has had enough. Gently squeeze baby's feet when the swing comes toward you. Hide your face with your hands and say "boo" as you lean in to push. Simply sitting in the swing and kicking his legs is great fun for baby. As baby grows and becomes an accomplished baby swinger, you may hear the words, "high, high, high." That means keep on pushing!

the sandbox scene

Ages: 18 months and up

A well-planned sandy area at a park is a great place for baby to explore. There are endless possibilities and only one rule to remember: don't throw sand! While baby  is practicing digging, filling, and pouring, she also will have opportunities to watch other babies playing. Baby's first attempts at socializing outside the family just might occur in the sandbox. Some useful items for sand play include:

- Shoebox to fill and dump
- Frozen juice containers for filling and making towers
- Sand shovel, spoons, ice cream scooper
- Measuring cups
- Variety of vehicles and plastic figures

Make a hill of sand with baby. Pat it down all around, then, starting at opposite sides, dig through trying to reach each other's hands. Play hide-and-seek with toy animals by burying them under the sand, then trying to find them. Smooth out an area of sand and make hand and footprints. Dig a hole and fill it with water, then watch the water disappear. If the weather is warm, bury each other's feet.

tiny treasure hunt

Ages: 12 months and up

Materials
Sand shovel or spoon
Yarn or string
Coffee can, cookie tin, or small shoe box
Costume jewelry (anything treasure-like)

Place jewelry in a container and hide it under some leaves, near a bush, behind a tree, or in a small hole covered with sand or dirt. Create a paper or yarn trail by tying yarn around or onto trees, bushes, and play equipment. Lay a few pieces of yarn on the ground too. You may have to be sneaky, setting this up while baby is occupied with a toy in the sand, or swinging in a baby swing. Hide the treasure close by so you'll be able to see baby at all times as he searches for the treasure. When you and baby are ready say, "Let's go on a treasure hunt, yarn marks the trail." Pick up the yarn as you move from place to place. If you like, make up a story about pirates leaving the treasure a long time ago.

five, six, pick-up sticks

Ages: 18 months and up

Materials
Pail, paper bag, or shoe box

Use a pail to help baby collect interesting nature items. Twigs, sticks, wood chips, leaves, sand, shells, pebbles, and nuts are all fair game as baby explores the park. Once collected, dump everything on a smooth surface and encourage baby to talk about the collection. Which stick or pebble is the biggest? Which is the smallest? Are some things smooth, rough, wet, or dry? Arrange and rearrange your found items with baby according to the characteristics of what you find.

★ **Wit & Wisdom** ★

To keep the temperature down in the kid's wading pool on hot summer days, I make blocks of ice by freezing water in milk cartons. Then I cut out the frozen blocks and drop them into the pool. The kids also love watching them disappear.
—Carla S., Atlanta, Georgia

baby soccer

Ages: 18 months and up

Materials
Blanket
Soft ball

Baby will love to kick a ball, even if he doesn't have the coordination to swing his leg on his own. Set up a goal about twenty feet away from baby using rocks, sticks, or toys as markers. Hold baby under his armpits and swing him toward the ball so that his legs kick the ball. Pretend you are playing a soccer game. Follow the ball to wherever it lands and swing baby to kick the ball again. If you have other children, they might even be defenders trying to kick the ball the other way. Run with baby to get the ball and continue kicking until the ball goes into the goal. Cheer baby on for the points scored!

★ Wit & Wisdom ★

My eighteen-month-old daughter loves to walk our black lab, but she can't do it alone. So I decided to put two leashes on our dog; I hold one and she holds one. Dog walking has become our special father-daughter time.
—Pete H., Alexandria, Virginia

blanket games

Don't ever forget to bring the blanket to the park, it's great to sit on and play with.

Parachute toys: This game is fun to play with three or more, so ask a few kids at the park to join in. Grab the corners of the blanket. Put a toy in the middle of the blanket and propel it into the air as you all lift the blanket up. Catch the toy as the blanket is lowered.

Blanket float: Holding the edge of the blanket, everyone raises the blanket in the air and quickly tries to get under it as the blanket falls on your heads.

Rolling up, rolling out: Let baby lie on the blanket with head over the edge. Begin rolling baby up, making sure her head is sticking out. Make sure the grass where you are rolling baby up is soft without rocks or sticks. Once baby is rolled up, hold onto the edge and let baby unroll. Do this slowly until baby gets used to it, then increase the speed.

★ Wit & Wisdom ★

The one toy I made sure to have in my diaper bag whenever I went anywhere was a bottle of bubbles. No matter where we were, my daughter would be totally excited when I took them out.
—Mirna H., Los Angeles, California

touch adventure

This activity can be done wherever you are with baby—inside, outside, in the car, at stores, or in restaurants. Take baby's hand and place it on an object. Name and describe the object. Don't worry if baby pulls away from the object, some babies want to look at an object first for a while before touching it. Then describe the object using colorful adjectives.

When baby gets older, make a guessing game out of it by closing your eyes and trying to guess what is being touched.

233

★ Wit & Wisdom ★

To keep baby's bottle cool on a hot day, fill a bottle with a few ounces of water, cap it, and put it in the freezer. Add the juice or water before you go out and the bottle will stay cool as the ice inside it melts.
—Amanda P., Aspen, Colorado

what's yours is mine

Park time with baby can be frustrating if your baby continually wanders over to other babies nearby, sits down next to them, and begins playing with their toys. At this stage, baby thinks that she can have everything she sees, and she wants to explore everything around her. Here are a few tips to make park play easier:

- Practice going to the park with another parent and child to teach your baby how to share with another baby without grabbing things.
- Approach any mother at the park and introduce yourself to break the ice. Then both of you can direct the babies' play.
- Make sure you bring toys to the park that your baby likes to play with. She can then take one of her toys to show the other baby.
- Wrap one of baby's old toys she hasn't seen for a while in bright paper and give it to her as a surprise.

After a few trips to the park, both you and baby will have made a few new friends.

backyard beasts

Protect baby from the sun and bug bites with these tips:

To avoid bug bites:
- Dress your child appropriately; wear light-colored clothing (bright colors attracts bugs), if walking in brush areas, wear long pants, long-sleeved shirts, socks, and shoes. Make sure your child does not wash with scented soaps or use scented lotions, which also attract bugs.
- Be wary of sunscreen-insect repellent combinations. These are fine for one application, but reapplying, which you may need to do for the sunscreen, may cause overexposure to deet (an ingredient in most bug repellents).
- Treat minor bug bites promptly by applying an ice cube to reduce swelling and minimize itching. Hydrocortisone cream can also be used.
- Extreme swelling, trouble breathing, hives, swollen tongue, headache, or nausea may indicate a life-threatening allergic reaction—in these cases seek immediate medical attention.

To protect kids from the sun:
- Use a total protection approach, which includes a broad-spectrum water-proof sunscreen of 15 or higher, wearing protective clothing like hats, sunglasses, and other clothing designed to screen out the sun. Also avoid direct sunlight whenever possible between 10 a.m. and 4 p.m.
- Put sunscreen on your children before they go outside—most sunscreens take 15 minutes before they begin to work.
- Even if your sunscreen claims to be all-day and waterproof, reapply it at least once during the day.

celebrations

neighborhood welcome

There may be new mothers in your neighborhood you have never met. How fun it would be to invite them over for tea and snacks. Pick a date for your welcome tea and write up a little flyer inviting all mothers with children under five years to attend. Put the flyer in the mailboxes near your house. Hire a baby-sitter to watch the children so the mothers can visit. Name tags are a must for the children and the mothers. Put a notebook out for everyone to list their name, address, phone number, children's names and ages, and whether they would be interested in meeting to play regularly at someone's home or a park. Think about the resource mothers can be for each other. This could lead to a neighborhood child-care co-op, car pool possibilities, resources for doctors, baby-sitters, etc. Most of all, it is important to have friends that live close who can be supportive. Send a copy of the name list to each person after the event.

baby sleeps through the night

Celebrate baby sleeping through the night for the first time. The day after the big sleep, plan to have a night walk as a family. Night is a mysterious and beautiful time with many new sounds. It is an adventure everyone can look forward to, especially big brothers and sisters. Bring a thermos of hot chocolate and a blanket so everyone can stop and sit somewhere to look at the stars. The fresh air will most likely guarantee baby will repeat the previous night by sleeping until morning! Sweet dreams...

sibling party

When baby is one month old, invite other mothers with young children your older child's age over for a celebration. Make sure all babies are left at home and that the new baby in your house is being looked after by someone else. Plan games according to the ages of children attending (see the Child Care and Playgroup chapter for game ideas). Focus on the baby's siblings. Point out to them that the reason for the celebration is that they are so special. All children should receive a prize of some sort. Have fun with the older child, making no mention of baby at all.

baby's birthday

Baby might not understand what a birthday is until his second or third year but he will certainly feel the excitement of something special happening to him if any of the following events happen.

1. Before baby wakes, maybe even the night before, decorate baby's room with balloons, streamers, confetti, etc.
2. Put a present in baby's bed so upon awakening baby can open it. If baby is too young to open it, leave a rattle or toy with bright ribbon around it.
3. Buy a plain white sheet to be used as a birthday tablecloth. Have all the guests sign it in permanent ink. This sheet can be washed and used year after year. Or use finger paints and a large piece of craft paper. Let everyone make a handprint and then sign it. Hang this on baby's wall.
4. Start a birthday journal. Have each member of the family write a story about baby and any events that happened during that year, or create a special message or drawing for baby. Each year add to this birthday journal.
5. Ask each of baby's grandparents to write a letter to him on his birthday each year. Save these and give them to baby when he grows up.
6. Serve assorted baby foods for dinner. Baby will laugh to see everyone eating the same thing as he is.

birthday theme ideas

Babies that are ages one and two will enjoy having a party with other children, as long as no one plays with their toys, and you have a parent attending for each child. It can be fun to have a theme party, which means all the games, decorations, and food follow the same idea. Here are a few baby themes:

Trains, Trucks, Buses, or Planes: Decorations could be toys or trucks. Have everyone make a shoe box train and pull it around. Babies could get conductor hats as party favors, and the cake could represent a wheel.

Balls: All the games could have to do with balls. For an invitation, write the party information on a small rubber ball and give it to the child.

Dolls: Decorate in tea party fashion, have each child bring a doll. Serve small sandwiches the dolls can share and tea served in tiny cups. Give a piece of doll clothing as a party favor. Make a cake using a rounded jelly mold, then stick an old Barbie in it. Then decorate the cake like a skirt.

Blocks: Have games around building with blocks. Use big cardboard blocks and boxes to make an obstacle course or fort for babies to play in. Even the cake can be cut, stacked, and iced to look like blocks.

pass the parcel

Materials
Candy
Wrapping paper
Small gifts
Music

Children of all ages love playing this game at parties and celebrations. Wrap up one prize or candy. Then wrap another one over the top of the first. Keep adding gifts and candy in layers until you have one large parcel.

When it's time to play, everyone sits in a circle (if babies are very small, parents can hold them on their laps). Someone needs to be in charge of the music. Turn the music on and begin passing the parcel. When it has gone around at least once, turn the music off. Whoever is holding the parcel gets to open one layer of paper, getting a prize. The music person needs to make sure that everyone gets at least one prize.

baby things exchange party

Invite all your friends and neighbors over for an informal exchange of unwanted baby things. Items could include clothes, books, toys, blankets, crib or room accessories. Most baby items are used for such a short period of time it saves money if everyone shares. You could also set up a lend table where people could write down things like baby swings or infant seats that they are not using right now, but want returned. If you want to make a game out of it, set the items up like an auction, giving poker chips out at the door based on the value of the items being donated. People could then purchase or bid on items according to the chips they have.

thanksgiving box

Materials
Shoe box
Decorations: paint, paper, markers, etc.

Decorate the shoe box and cut a slit in the top large enough to fit folded pieces of paper. Put a small pile of scrap paper and a pen next to the box. Write anything that happens that you are thankful for and place the notes in the box. All family members can contribute to the box. You can even write things for baby, like, "I'm thankful I can finally eat solid food." On Thanksgiving or another celebrated day, read all the slips in the box. Remember to write in the little daily things that occur. They will bring a smile to everyone's face as they rekindle memories.

winter picnic

Pick a day in the middle of winter when everyone in the family is sick of staying indoors. Make a summer-style picnic. Gather soft balls that can be thrown in the house without destroying everything, and get out favorite games. Lay out a large tablecloth on the family room floor and get ready to munch.

While lunching, share favorite summer memories. Baby is sure to love this style of eating, since all her favorite people are at eye level. It may be so much fun that a weekly picnic could be planned!

★ Wit & Wisdom ★

When a big winter storm hit, my son desperately wanted to go outside and play in the snow, but it was way too cold. Instead, I went outside and gathered three big bowls of snow. We built a miniature snowman on the kitchen table. It's become our winter tradition.
—JoAnn W., Lakeshore, Wisconsin

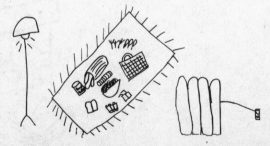

sing along

Materials
Music baby has heard many times
Words to a few of the songs written down for family members
Homemade instruments: drum, tambourine, or bells

Make sure baby is on the same level as everyone else, either in a high chair while everyone sits around the table, or all sitting on the floor. Put the music on and have everyone sing softly with it. As baby gets used to it and starts to smile, add instruments, arm movements, and clapping hands. Baby will feel the joy and will be thrilled to be included in the group fun.

christmas morning

Here's a tradition to start on baby's first Christmas, since, as baby grows older, it may mean you sleep until 7 a.m. instead of 5 a.m. on Christmas morning! Fill baby's stocking full of small presents that can be looked at and played with without your assistance. Baby will wake up, see the stocking, and be delightfully surprised. You may want to make this a birthday tradition as well. Surprises are fun for you and baby and can create wonderful memories!

★ Wit & Wisdom ★

Don't knock yourself out getting great or expensive holiday or birthday presents. I found my baby was just as happy to open empty boxes, and since she had no idea what to expect, she was happy with the excitement of the celebration.
—Sue, Tifton, Georgia

the way we were

Invite friends over who have children. Ask everyone to bring ten pictures of themselves before they had children. One or two couples at a time get to play the Newlywed Game. Using the pictures to spark ideas, the audience creates ten questions. One partner goes out of the room while the other answers the questions. Then the out-of-room partner comes in and tries to guess how the other answered the questions. The couple that gets the most questions correct wins. Here are a few hard to remember funny questions: When and where was your first kiss? What color is your wife's bathrobe? Where is the most unusual place you have made love? Who was your best friend in grade school? What is your favorite thing to do? What would be your ideal date? Be creative in creating the questions and have fun!

baby shower games

Instant Memory Book: This is a great keepsake for mom-to-be that involves all of the shower guests and doesn't take much extra time. You'll need an album or scrapbook with blank pages, Instant Polaroid camera, three packs of Polaroid film, a glue stick, and tape. During the party, take lots of photos with the camera; glue them in right away and write short, funny captions for them. Remember to take pictures during the games and record in the book who won!

Baby Relay: Have enough baby dolls for each player. If you don't want to buy them ask women who already have children to bring extra dolls for you. Lay each doll, undressed, next to a diaper. On the other side of the room, lay out enough empty baby bottles (or play bottles) for each player. Each player must diaper their baby, run across and "feed" baby, then run back and "burp" baby. The first person finished wins the game.

Price Is Right Game: Line up various baby supplies. Have people guess the price. The closest wins ten points per item.

Bottle Race: Fill small baby bottles with juice. Divide into teams of four people. Each person on the team gets a baby bottle. This is a race to see which team finishes their bottles first! Begin with the first person, when she finishes, the next begins and so on until the last person finishes.

Carpenter's Convention: Why should men be excluded from having their own baby shower? Write the invitation on a piece of paper and then glue it to a piece of scrap wood. This is actually a construction party where the men will assemble furniture, or whatever else needs to be put together for the baby's room. If the group wants to build a piece of furniture, make sure to have a pattern and supplies ready. Play favorite music, serve great food, and don't forget the beer!

husband's turn to serve

OK dad, it's time for you to plan a party your wife will love! Invite a few couples over, making sure the men involved talk beforehand about the theme. Make a list of ten things the men decide together that their wives would like: a foot or back massage, a walk in the garden, a dance, or a poem recited. Put each idea in a hat and let each woman pick from the hat. Then, her own husband has to do what is on the piece of paper. Of course, the men make dinner and clean up as well, so the women can sit back, relax, and talk. It's worth it, guys, she'll always remember it!

★ Wit & Wisdom ★

When my wife told me it would be fun to plan a play date with another dad or two and their babies, I thought that other guys would think I was weird. But I now have a weekend playgroup with a bunch of dads— we talk about dad stuff and have a great time.
—Brian, St. Paul, Oregon

family growth

point of view

Do you find yourself feeling your home isn't what it used to be, that things look messy and toys are everywhere? Well, there is no known way to eliminate the disorder, so the best thing to do is change your point of view! Sit down and talk as a couple about how the changes affect each of you. If possible, provide a play area for your child where toys can be put away, and put up objects that could hurt baby or that baby could break. Most babies seem to have toys occupying space in every room of the house. If both of you can accept this as something that will pass, you will both be happier and your expectations will not bring unnecessary pressure.

★ Wit & Wisdom ★

I found a way to squelch my anxiety over having a clean house. I give myself thirty minutes every day to clean up something. These are the kind of cleaning projects like a closet, mopping a floor—things you don't do daily. It is really amazing how much I get done over a period of time.
—Gretchen, Gustavus, Alaska

family journal

Find a place to put a large blank book so family members know where it is and will be encouraged to write regularly. This blank book can be used as a daily diary or as a special events book. Children too young to write can dictate stories and draw handprints. Those too young to talk can be represented by weekly pictures with descriptions of new things they can do. The book can contain all aspects of family life. Visitors can write their names and a little about their visits, children can write their Christmas or birthday wish lists. Baby's first words can be recorded. Pictures drawn at school can be glued in. We guarantee this book will be a sought-after treasure in years to come.

★ Wit & Wisdom ★

Our daughter learned to brush her teeth by mimicking me. Either face to face or with both of us facing the mirror, she loves brushing away, just like her daddy.
—James, Baton Rouge, Louisiana

perfect imperfection

Everyone needs to feel pleased with themselves and family members can help each other by pointing out good efforts. Don't make the mistake of waiting for someone to do something perfectly before you say something positive. Today, tell your child or spouse something you think they do well, something you can both be proud of. Take a minute to think of all the things you do in your own life. Can you feel satisfied with a few things in your life without expecting perfection? Recognizing your own perfect imperfection and calling attention to the positive things family members do will increase everyone's feelings of self-esteem. Do this for two weeks without missing a day and see what changes you notice.

family postcards

On baby's birth announcement or the next time you mail out holiday cards to family and friends, ask each family to send baby a postcard of their hometown with a special note written especially for baby. Put the postcards in a photo book for baby to look at and save. When the postcards come in, talk to baby about who sent them. Keep up baby's postcard book by sending and encouraging others to send postcards from their home or travels.

★ Wit & Wisdom ★

I send very special cards to my parents. I write a note saying happy birthday, get well soon, missing you, or thank you and put the note in front of my son so it looks like he is holding it. Then I take a picture and send that made into a note card.
—Josie B., Las Vegas, Nevada

253

teach compassion

If you want to teach baby compassion you have to model it. If he watches you reaching out to help people he will grow up doing the same. Here are a few ideas:

- Let someone in the grocery store go ahead of you if they have less or seem to be in a hurry. Offer to carry someone's groceries out to the car.
- Help other parents who might be struggling with their kids, on a plane or at a restaurant. (They may need a trip to the bathroom, but have nobody to hold the baby.)
- Make dinner for a sick neighbor.
- Say hello and smile at people you pass!
- Give food to the homeless.
- Make only positive comments about people who are different from you.
- Go through baby's toy box yearly and donate all half of the toys to charity.

do nothing day

Pick one day a month as a "do nothing day." Everyone is free from chores, sort of like a sick day without being sick. Rooms stay messy while everyone does exactly what they want. This might be a good night to plan dinner out as a family. Of course, with babies some things have to be done, but eliminate as many of the other chores as possible. This is a great family tradition, and as children grow it encourages them to be more responsible for themselves on these special days.

love letter

With a new baby around, you and your spouse may have less time to spend alone together and less time to express your love for each other. So, don't wait for Valentine's Day to write a love letter to your spouse. Most of us feel silly writing love letters, but we all blush upon receiving one as we proceed to read the letter over and over! Letters are one of the best ways to say something you might be too embarrassed to say in person. For a little fun, add a few gift vouchers, made and performed by you, for things you know your partner likes. Be creative and remember to keep the romance alive!

family photo game

Go through photo albums to get pictures of grandma, grandpa, aunts, uncles, and cousins. Take photos of mom, dad, brothers, and sisters. Laminate the photos and stick Velcro onto the back of them. Have baby touch, point to kiss, or whatever you tell her to do to or with the photo. You can tell her to put Uncle Jim on the table, or put cousin Lucy in the box, or put the dog next to Mom. In time, baby will know all the family faces!

★ **Wit & Wisdom** ★

I wanted to help my son at least recognize his grandma when she came to stay with us. So I put together a five-minute video of her and played it every day for a few weeks. When she arrived, he went right to her.
—Betty C., Ft. Lauderdale, Florida

surprise

Surprises are so much fun to give and to receive. Pick a day and time to surprise your mate. Here are a few suggestions:

- Hire a baby-sitter and take your mate out for a meal, movie, or dancing.
- Buy a small gift for no reason and put it on your mate's pillow.
- Invite a friend over you know he'd like to see, buy a special dessert for the visit, then leave them alone to talk.
- Make reservations at a hotel for the night and leave a message for her to meet you.

Be creative! You know what your partner likes, so take the time to do it now and then. You'll both reap the benefits.

thirty-minute talk

The following exercise is guaranteed to improve your marriage, no matter how good it already is! It's amazing how much you will each look forward to this special time. Pick a time that is convenient for both of you that can be kept like an appointment each day. Set a timer for fifteen minutes and one of you begin to talk about whatever you want: your day, problems, work, your relationship, kids, a hobby, etc. The other person just listens. Switch after fifteen minutes so you each get fifteen minutes of uninterrupted talk.

video moments

Rent or borrow a video camera if you don't own one, and recruit an assistant to help you if you can. Decide what everyday activities you will record and find your props. Record a day in the life of your baby. Start the video early in the morning while baby is still sleeping, catch baby waking up, getting dressed, eating, playing, riding in the car, walking, or in the stroller. Record baby with siblings or friends and follow baby all day through bathtime until bedtime. Make sure you have someone to help so you can be recorded with baby! Do a video day every six months, adding to the same tape each time. Baby will enjoy watching this as he grows, and will be thrilled with it when he has children of his own!

play date

Sometimes as adults we forget how to play with each other. So much time is spent working, dealing with kids, discussing finances, and coping with life, there seems to be no time to play. Play is important. It keeps the spirit alive and it reminds us that life is fun. Decide on a time when you will let yourself play. Go someplace with your partner like a bowling alley, a golf course, a swimming pool, etc. Laugh together, be silly, imagine, and dream. Declare one night a week as game night at home; play cards, charades, or a board game everyone likes. Make having fun together a priority!

nurse duty

If someone in your family isn't feeling well, create and post a "nurse duty" schedule. Nurse duty might include bringing in a glass of water, making lunch, adjusting blankets, reading a book, talking to pass the time, or taking baby out of mom's bed so that she can get some rest! Children can learn at a very young age that your family values taking care of each other. Very young children can be brought into the room to do things like rub feet or hands, help straighten the blanket, or hand mom, dad, brother, or sister a treat.

262

★ Wit & Wisdom ★

Please name and date baby pictures. Believe it or not, memories do fade and when there is more than one child, sometimes confusion arises.
—Sandy W., Galesburg, Illinois

mom's time

what is a mother?

A mother is not replaceable in a child's heart. If you are holding this book in hand, there is a child in your life that you are mothering in some way. Have you ever taken the time to think about what an amazing job it is to be a mother? What is a mother to you? What did you receive from your mother that you want to pass on to your child? What did you wish you had received? What are your dreams as a mother? Who are you to your child? Take fifteen minutes to think and write about what it means to be a mother.

tea for you

Take time out for a few minutes of calm at least once a day. Make a cup of hot tea or coffee, take the phone off the hook, and just relax. Read a good magazine article or shut your eyes and daydream. Don't get up for at least fifteen minutes, no matter what!

Note: One of the most beautiful compilations of original lullabies we have found is entitled *From a Mother's Heart* by Liliana Kohann. The lyrics deal with concepts such as love and self-esteem, and melodies are gorgeous. For information contact ArtPeace Music at LpArtPeace@aol.com.

surrender control

In order for mother to have some time to herself, other people have to help. That means things may not be done exactly as mother wishes. Clothes may be folded and put in the wrong piles, the dishwasher might be loaded out of order, or your mail might be mixed up. Practice surrendering control. For one week let your husband, mother, friend, or baby-sitter do things their way. Just sit back and enjoy the fact that *you* are not doing them.

★ Wit & Wisdom ★

My three girlfriends and I have ten children between us. One day we were complaining that we could never get our houses cleaned. So we decided to clean one of our houses each week. The catch is that the person whose house is being cleaned watches the kids and makes everyone lunch. It is much more fun to clean someone else's house!
—Bridgette W., Boulder, Colorado

vision poster

Materials
Old magazines
Scissors
Glue
Poster board

Take an evening to make a poster with pictures that represent things you want in your life. Look through magazines to find pictures that represent your "vision" of what you want your life to be: a couple embracing could mean a close relationship, or a picture of a baby might mean another child. Hang this poster where you can see it often: a closet or bathroom door works well. It's inspiring to focus on possibilities.

★ Wit & Wisdom ★

I read a quote from Theodore Roosevelt a few years ago and it has become my motto: "Whenever you are asked if you can do a job, tell 'em, 'Certainly, I can!' Then get busy and find out how to do it."
—Annie H., Dallas, Texas

write it now

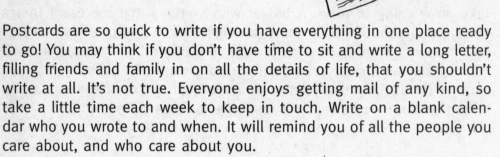

Materials
All sorts of postcards
Blank note cards
Calendar book
Assorted pretty stamps
Basket or box

Postcards are so quick to write if you have everything in one place ready to go! You may think if you don't have time to sit and write a long letter, filling friends and family in on all the details of life, that you shouldn't write at all. It's not true. Everyone enjoys getting mail of any kind, so take a little time each week to keep in touch. Write on a blank calendar who you wrote to and when. It will remind you of all the people you care about, and who care about you.

role models

In olden days, older and wiser women in the family passed down skill and knowledge to new mothers. Today, extended families live farther apart, so new mothers are left to fend for themselves without the timeless advice of elders. Yet role models do exist in your community and within your circle of friends. Take a few minutes and think about the women you know that you admire for some reason. Would you feel comfortable asking them for advice or discussing your fears? It is important to reach out and be open to learning new skills. Tell someone you admire that you see her as a role model, and ask her if she would mind you asking her for advice and support on a regular basis. There is no greater compliment for the woman you ask, so be brave and reach out!

fun time

It is important for a mom to find time to do fun things for herself; otherwise, she gets worn out, and loses enthusiasm for life. Forget that you barely have time to brush your teeth, and take the time to make a list of things that are fun for you. Things as simple as a thirty-minute uninterrupted phone call count when you're a mom! Make sure the list includes as many fun things as you can think of. Post the list somewhere you will see it everyday. Here is the hard part: allow yourself to do one item on the list every day without feeling guilt that you should be doing something else. As children grow, it is important for them to see that mom values herself. Your children will respect you for respecting yourself, as well as learning to value their own needs by modeling your behavior. Everyone wins, so have some fun!

jazz clean

Each day some time is spent tidying up the house, even if you don't want to. So why not make it a fun hour of exercise and music? Put on your tennis shoes and workout gear. When you bend to pick something up, do twenty pliés. Run from room to room, or do jumping jacks and leg kicks. While on the floor, do a few sit-ups and push-ups. Fold clothes while doing standing leg lifts. Playing your favorite music loudly, just move, dance, and breathe. Set an amount of time you want to devote to cleaning and don't go over it. Save the rest to do tomorrow!

learn it together

Put together a list of other mothers you know. Decide on something you would all like to learn, like first aid, baby massage, beauty makeover, or yoga. Send invitations or print up flyers to invite other mothers to the event. Hire someone to come and teach the class. If the cost is more than you want to spend, state on the invitation that there will be a charge. Don't worry, nobody will mind chipping in, and besides, if it's a subject that interests you, chances are other mothers will enjoy learning it too. You may want to hire a baby-sitter for everyone to share. On the day of the event, serve coffee, tea, or juice and something simple, like muffins, bagels, or cookies. If it goes well, maybe you could discuss doing another one. Get someone else to volunteer to organize the next event. Who knows? This may become a monthly meeting.

buy flowers

Flowers make a home feel alive, happy, and bright. They refresh the spirit! If you have flowers in your yard, pick them often, and if not, buy some from the farmers market once in a while. Even branches with pretty fall leaves will work if you are on a budget. Gaze at the flowers throughout the day, and pick off the dead buds and rearrange into appropriate vases during the week. Every effort made to make daily life special is an affirmation that you are important and worth spending time on.

★ **Wit & Wisdom** ★

I used to find myself saying that this or that was a waste of money, until one day I found that I was always referring to the things that would have made me happy. Now I try to indulge my own needs at least some of the time.
—Austin, Pittsfield, Massachusetts

special photo album

Every time a roll of film is developed, there always seems to be one picture you stare at in awe. It captures your child, a favorite memory, or an unforgettable event so perfectly. Buy a beautiful picture album more decorative than the family's ordinary one. Put that special photo memory in it. You will never have to waste time rummaging through piles of pictures to find that special one. It may take ten years to fill it up, but in the end it will be your prized possession.

time to organize

With small children, life has to be simplified in order to survive! Start by committing one day each month to organizing some part of your life. Start with your closet. Try everything on to see what still fits. If you haven't worn something in a year, give it away. Try to pick two or three colors that your wardrobe revolves around. This makes dressing much easier, and saves money on accessories! So your closet doesn't look packed, box up seasonal clothes, adding scented soap to the box for freshness upon opening. Do this closet cleaning at least twice a year. To save time, buy your underwear and nylons two times a year. Shop from catalogs after baby is asleep. Look forward to organization day each month and don't feel guilty in between dates—you will get to it on schedule.

makeover magic

Moms need their makeup on and hair done in less than fifteen minutes, am I right? It's worth putting a little extra effort and practice into getting a quick routine in place. If you've convinced yourself you don't care what you look like because no one will see you, you're missing out on the simple joy of feeling good about yourself. *You* will see you, and that counts! If you look a mess you'll most likely feel a mess. Even while wearing a sweat suit you can look put together. Go get a makeover and make sure to tell the makeup artist that you need a makeup routine that you can do in seven minutes. Bring your own makeup so you won't be tempted to buy everything they use. It's also a good idea to pick an easy hairstyle that can be complete in under ten minutes as well. You'll feel great about the new you!

weekend escape

With or without your partner, you must get away from it all every so often. The word *vacation* comes from the Latin word *vacatio*, which means freedom, to be empty, or release from occupation. Take two days and stay in a hotel or country inn near where you live. Order room service, see a play, act as if you took a plane and traveled very far for a vacation. After just two days, you will return refreshed with new energy.

★ Wit & Wisdom ★

Baby sign language really works! Don't worry about the whole big system if you don't have the time or energy. We found it helpful and rewarding to teach just a few simple signs revolving around eating, like "more" and "milk."
—Isabella, Duluth, Minnesota

dad's time

baby's world

277

If you're a dad who works every day, not having as much time as you would like to spend with a child, try this: spend at least thirty minutes with your baby doing nothing but being there. Follow baby no matter what he does—if he crawls, crawl along; if he babbles, babble back; if he wants to sing a song, clap along. What does the world look like at baby's eye level? The idea is for you to let the child direct you, and for you to step into the child's world. This is a great bonding experience to do with older children as well. In fact, if you do this once a week until they leave home, you have given your child an amazing gift...you paid attention!

★ Wit & Wisdom ★

One of my favorite things to do is read. Whenever my six-month-old son gets fussy and wants my attention I read whatever I enjoy reading to him. That way I get to do something I enjoy and he totally enjoys hearing my voice.
—Jack S., Houston, Texas

what is a father?

Take a few minutes out of your day to think about your father, his strengths, weaknesses, the time you spent together, and what he taught you about life. What kind of father do you want to be? Write down your goals as a father. Who do you want to be to your child? What do you want to teach him or her? How do you plan on showing your love and concern each day?

★ **Wit & Wisdom** ★

The presents my father most appreciated were the bookmarks I made for him out of the grandchildren's photographs. I simply laminated them.
—Brennan T., Lake Tahoe, California

another dad

Make the effort to become friends with another man who also has a baby. Look around at work, at the gym, the park, or wherever you spend time. Dads need support too; life has changed, and you need to learn a new role. This friend you find will be going through similar changes in his life, so walk the path together. Plan trips together to the park, zoo, or lake. Make it a point to talk about the feelings you have, your concerns as a new father, and how your life has changed since having a child.

★ Wit & Wisdom ★

Whenever I take my kids to events where we have seats, I pin their ticket stubs to their shirts so that if they get lost, the usher can bring them back.
—Dennis P., Boulder, Colorado

mother and wife

The woman in your life plays the roles of wife, mother, and lover. Take a few minutes to examine how you see her in each of these roles. Do you give encouragement and support her in each of these roles, or do you emphasize one role more than another? Do you make time for her in each of her roles? Do you tell her what you need from her in each of these roles? Take time today to tell her that you see her as all these women, and that you love every aspect of her.

★ Wit & Wisdom ★

One of my husband's favorite surprises is when I pack a picnic lunch, bring the boys with me to his office, and kidnap him for an hour's peace sitting on a blanket in the grass at a nearby park.
—Rhonda G., Ashland, Oregon

reality to fantasy

What would your life be like if you lived in a castle? What would you do if you were president? How would you feel if you were the world's best at something? What would you do with millions of dollars? Write down all of your thoughts. Visualizing yourself having great wealth, success, or happiness will bring a smile to your face. The point is that it's fun to dream, to step out of reality and into fantasy once in a while.

★ **Wit & Wisdom** ★

A good friend once told me that if you have no dreams you have no direction for the journey that is your life. Now I try to dream big so at least I know where I want to be headed.
—Pam, Camden, Maine

dad things

Some things dads just seem to do better than moms; things like wrestling, rolling in the leaves, fishing, galloping around the house, and washing the car. Make a mental list of the things you like to do with baby that mom doesn't really care to do. Make an extra effort to do these things with baby. Special time with dad is very important.

★ Wit & Wisdom ★

My wife and I swear by the "sleep sacks" that are popular in Europe. Once our daughter outgrew swaddling, we always worried about her being out from under her blankets. Now we don't have to chase those blankets around the crib at night anymore!
—Todd, Lombard, Illinois

who are you?

Do you have hobbies or special interests? It is important that as baby grows he really knows you. What better way than to share with him things you like to do? Start early. When you pick out books at the library, pick them on subjects that interest you, then share your joy. When you go someplace special, bring baby along. Point out things you like. Make silly jokes. Talk about your work when you get home, telling baby what you do all day. Of course, you also have to reciprocate and express interest in baby's life!

box forts

Materials
Lots of old boxes
Sheet or blanket
Rubber bands

Here's a fun inside or outside, all-day activity. So many exciting things can be done with old boxes if you have lots of imagination. Design a masterpiece: use boxes with a sheet over the top to make a tunnel, fasten the sheets to chair tops with rubber bands to make a tent, stack boxes high to make towers, or crawl inside boxes to hide. If baby gets tired of crawling in and out of boxes, she can crawl over and under dad, her own man-made bridge and tunnel!

★ **Wit & Wisdom** ★
I keep several water-filled balloons in the freezer, just in case of a bump or bruise. Make sure to wrap it in a towel first.
—Paul W., Nashville, Tennessee

junk mailman

As you sort through your mail and pay your bills, let baby sit beside you and open all of the junk mail. Babies love to rip paper (be careful of paper cuts). This will keep them occupied for as long as you need to go through your bills. You may even have time to read the paper! If baby is old enough, you can also pretend to be mail carriers going out to the mailbox, then delivering mail to people.

shoe box train

Materials
Old shoe boxes (5 or 6)
String or twine

Babies love to pull things. Dad, this is your project, since construction and sound effects are usually a specialty! String the shoe boxes together using whatever creative sewing pattern you can come up with so the boxes will stay behind each other in a straight line when you pull. Start at the last box and work forward, tying the end so baby has a handle to pull.

Once the train is made, put a few of baby's small toys in it. If you have a train whistle, blow it; if not, you'll have to pretend you're the conductor making all the appropriate sounds.

talk about feelings

It's very important that you talk to your wife about how it feels to be a dad. In fact, it would be a good idea if you took the time to write your wife a letter telling her what your new role means to you. Tell her all your feelings, the good and the not so good. Tell her how much you appreciate the little daily jobs she does. Tell her what a good mother she is. Reassure her that she is still as sexy as before the baby. Tell her what you need. When children are young, along with positive feedback, open communication is what will help you survive. Encourage each other to open up and express yourselves.

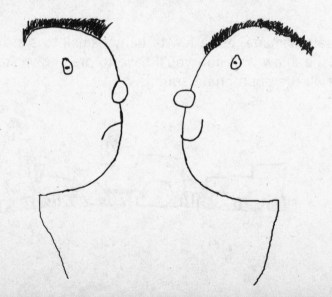

sex after baby

Life with baby often means less of a sex life. Everyone is exhausted by bedtime! Nobody will disagree with you that it's hard work to keep the passion alive in your relationship, but there are ways. Here are a few:

- Have an affair with your wife. Write her a sexually explicit love letter, then give her a time and place to meet you.
- Accept your wife's new body after she has a child. It is difficult for her to go through her own bodily changes. She will feel sexier if you are positive and supportive.
- Make weekly dates for sex. Take turns setting the scene. It will give you both something to look forward to and depend on.
- Every woman loves a massage, and it will most likely lead to something else.

siblings

you are great

Make sure your other children overhear you saying great things about them! So often when a new baby arrives the talk is all about baby, even though baby can't hear it or appreciate it. The older brother or sister is usually standing right there hearing all of the raving. So, tell a few of your friends and family the plan, which is to talk about your other children as well. Next time you are having tea or talking on the phone, talk about how much fun you have with them, what great things they are doing, and how lucky you are to have such great kids.

a picture of me

Materials
Picture of big brother or sister
Poster board
Markers
Stickers
Glue

Have the older child glue a picture of themselves to the poster board and decorate it however they would like. Write "Big Brother" or "Big Sister" on the board. Let the artist decide where in baby's room to hang his portrait. Make sure baby can see it often. Siblings can feel less important when they get less time and attention, especially if they have been the only child for a while. To help build an older child's self-esteem, include him in decisions about baby and repeatedly tell him how wonderful, important, and helpful he is. Frequent hugs are important too!

child's photo album

Materials
4" by 6" photo album
Current family photos

Whenever you have pictures developed, make sure to have two copies made. Brothers and sisters like having their very own picture albums full of pictures of THEM, so make sure you don't just take pictures of baby. Each time you get a roll of film developed, let your child pick out a few pictures she wants to add to her own album. This also gives her something to do while you are putting pictures in the family albums.

a hero's story

Spontaneously tell a story during a quiet time or at bedtime about baby's brother or sister. Build their self-esteem by bringing up all the things they do each day for you, for baby, at school, or playing. Make the sibling the hero in some way, someone baby and everyone else looks up to. Stories like this are fun because everyone can listen at the same time, baby is entertained, and big brothers and sisters feel very important. You may even want to tape record these stories since the heroes will love to hear them over and over again.

★ Wit & Wisdom ★

My five-year-old has a special game he plays with his one-year-old sister. They take a towel and each holds the end while I put a beach ball in the center so they can toss it up in the air and catch it in the towel. I get to be the one who retrieves the ball when it falls!
—Jessie S., Napa, California

big brother and sister shirts

Materials
Fabric pen
Fabric paint
Large sponge
White T-shirts
Large piece of cardboard to fit inside
T-shirt to stretch it out while being painted

Write the words "I'm the Big Brother" or "I'm the Big Sister" on the blank T-shirts and let them dry. Using one color of fabric paint at a time, pour a little fabric paint on top of the sponge and rub it around. Rub baby's foot on top of the sponge, then step it onto the shirt. Repeat with the same color for as many footprints as you like. Let older siblings help direct the design. Change the color on the sponge and make prints in other colors.

Note: Make a shirt for baby too that says, "Everyone loves me," and let the older siblings put their handprints on it!

how i feel

Materials
Sheet of butcher paper long enough to fit the tallest
  child's body outline
Crayons or markers

Have each child, including baby, lie on the sheet of butcher paper indi-
vidually. Take the marker or crayon and outline each body. Have each
sibling talk about how they feel about baby, how baby has changed
their lives for better or worse, what they like and dislike about baby,
and anything else you can think of. Write these things inside the outline of the baby. Be sure to let them know you understand all their feelings! Then ask the siblings how they think baby feels about them and
write this inside their outlines. It is important that everyone in a family
believes their feelings matter. New babies change the makeup of your
family, and talking about the changes helps everyone!

puppet theater

Materials
Refrigerator box
Paint
Fabric for curtains

An old refrigerator box makes a perfect puppet theater. The adult needs to do the cutting out, but after that, let the kids decorate. They will be so proud of their theater design and will be thrilled to have baby and parents attend opening night! First, tape any top or bottom flaps closed to make the box more sturdy. Stand the box up vertically, then cut a two-feet-tall hole at the very top of the box on the side that would face the audience. This will be the stage. Then, cut a three-feet-tall hole on the opposite side bottom so the children can crawl in. Let the kids design the outside. Staple fabric to the stage top and tie it at each side for curtains.

nature collage

Materials
Flat items found in nature: leaves, flower petals, grass, and feathers
Flat box lid
Glue
Paper

Have the older children point out to baby the kind of things to look for outside. Chances are baby will pull the whole flower out but that's OK; you can take the petals off later. Put all the collected items on the flat box lid. The adult or one of the siblings draws an outline of a butterfly, animal, or flower. Make this outline large and simple. Put glue directly onto the paper, small sections at a time. Help baby place the nature collectibles on the glued sections. Sometimes it is best to drop a flower petal and see where it lands.

Let dry and display for all to see.

homemade picture book

Materials
Magazines
Scissors
Glue
Construction paper—plain or colored,
  or a scrapbook with plain paper pages

Go through the magazine briefly with your older child, showing her
the kinds of pictures to cut out. Look for things that baby might recognize: animals, house, people, car, or plants. Cut out pictures and glue
them onto the paper or scrapbook. If your older child wants to, she can
write a word underneath each picture. It's also fun to put the pictures
in some sort of order that tells a story. Give the self-made picture book
to baby. This could be a special book that only the older brother or sister would be allowed to read or look at with baby.

handprint cookies

Materials
Cookie dough
Decorative frosting
Blunt knife

Roll dough out to about a quarter-inch thickness, then put the child's hand on top of the dough and cut around the outside. Make a few cookies for each child. If you would rather make small cookies, just use a thumbprint. Put them on a greased cookie sheet and bake. When cool, let children decorate the cookies. Babies love to feel soft, squishy things, so let them play with the dough, and help to roll it out. Then watch the fun as everyone decorates.

Cookie Dough Recipe:
½ cup brown sugar
2½ cups unbleached flour
½ cup butter
1 teaspoon vanilla
2 teaspoons baking powder
2 eggs
½ teaspoon salt

Directions
Cream sugar, butter, vanilla, and eggs. Mix in flour, baking powder, and salt. Chill dough for three hours. Preheat oven to 375°F (190°C). Roll dough out on floured surface. Cut with shaped cookie cutters. Bake seven to ten minutes. Yield: twenty-four cookies.

puppet pop-up

Baby likes to be surprised as he tries to guess where the puppets will pop up next. Give the older child a pile of puppets or stuffed animals. As baby sits in his high chair or other stationary place, have sibling pop the puppets out from behind her own back, from under a table, in front of the high chair tray. Try creating a repetitive pattern, having the puppet pop up from the right twice then the left once, and watch as baby begins to anticipate and predict where the puppet will pop up next. Encourage your older child to get creative with the ways she surprises baby. Babies also like to play this game with noisy toys.

ring of love

Materials
Your bodies, voices, and imagination
A room of any size

Move any pieces of furniture, toys, clothes, etc., out of the way so that you can hold hands and walk around in a circle (like ring around the rosie). The object of this activity is to have fun and at the same time give your child positive reinforcement. Hold hands and walk in a circle, first marching, then hopping, skipping, and running. Reverse direction often. As you do this, think of positive statements you could make, like, "We are nice and we can share," or "We love each other and we listen."

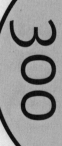

video visits

Is there a special place your baby especially likes to visit, like the zoo, a pet store, a toy store, or amusement park? Get your older child to help you make a video of your baby at that location. Maybe big brother or sister can be standing in front of the polar bear exhibit pointing to the mother bear as baby sits in the stroller, or maybe they could be sitting together on a baby ride at the amusement park. Make sure to video-tape all the surroundings that baby sees when she visits her favorite places. Baby does not have to be in every shot, it is more important to record the experience that baby has when she is there. On days when you cannot get out of the house for an adventure, put the tape in and let her watch it—with big brother or sister narrating, of course!

food fair

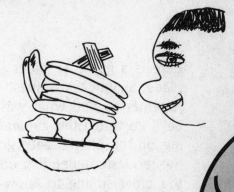

Materials
Assorted soft foods: finger food appropriate
 for baby, applesauce, or pudding
Plate
Bowls
High chair

Prepare yourself, baby, and older sibling, for food tasting and exploration. Have all foods on hand and ready to be eaten before starting. Place one type of food at a time on baby's tray and do the same on the other children's plates. Allow baby the freedom to explore the taste, smell, texture, size, sound, and temperature of each. Then give baby an opportunity to compare, by putting two or three different foods on his tray. Which one does baby eat first? Big brother and sister will also have a chance to do the food tasting and might have some suggestions of their own. Let older children put together original creations and see if baby will eat them. Enjoy what your little chefs create!

where's your bottle?

Here is a game an older sibling can play with baby, anytime and any-place. Simply ask a question or suggest an action, then go on a search together to find what was asked. For example: Where's your blanket? Let's go watch the gardener! What's in the toy box? Let's practice talk-ing on the phone. Let's go find the dog. Where is the garage? Change the requests depending on baby's abilities; of course, half the fun is for the older sibling to know the answer and help baby to find her way. Make sure baby doesn't just point to the object or action mentioned, the children have to go together to find it.

grandparenting

what do you need?

It's easy to remember how it felt to be exhausted from the work of parenting. When you go to visit your child, who is now a new parent, remember you are walking into her life and she may do things differently than you remember. Ask a few simple questions when you arrive so that you feel comfortable.

- The first and most important is "What can I do each day that will help you?" (For example, taking baby for a few hours each morning.)
- Could you write down the daily schedule?
- Is there a special way you do certain things, like the dishes, laundry, vacuuming, or playing with baby?
- Is there anything I should not do with baby?
- What does baby like?
- What are baby's habits and developmental level right now?

Think of any other questions that you want to ask, and remember that open communication will make the visit more enjoyable!

meet the neighborhood

Before the grandkids arrive, make a point to look for children in your neighborhood that look about the same age. Introduce yourself to their parents and tell them your grandchildren will be arriving soon for a visit. You might even be able to borrow toys, bikes, dolls, cribs, strollers, or car seats. Also, ask them to recommend a pediatrician and a baby-sitter so you will be prepared in case of emergency.

★ **Wit & Wisdom** ★

Whenever we go to visit my parents I let my mom know a week before we arrive what my daughter's favorite book is. She goes to the library or purchases that book and my daughter is always surprised that her grandparents know what her favorite book is and just happens to have it on hand.
—Marie S., Ephrata, Pennsylvania

establish a play area

If grandchildren will be spending time at your house, there are a few things you can do that will make visits more fun for everyone.

1. Start a separate cabinet where craft supplies are stored. The list should include crayons, paper, play dough, finger paint, old boxes, wrapping paper scraps, scissors, glue stick, old magazines, old socks, and felt.
2. Start a dress-up box. As you do your yearly closet cleaning, save the old jackets, dresses, high-heeled shoes, jewelry, hats, and ties. Consider cutting the dress bottoms and coat arms to a reasonable length.
3. Try to clean an area and designate it as a play area. Even a small area will do. This way there will be no excuse for having toys all over the house! Buy a cheap wall mirror and hang it up in this area, then watch the children find a million uses for it.
4. For inexpensive and instant room decoration the children will love, take a few photos of the kids and blow them up to poster size. Then, buy cheap plastic poster frames and hang them in the room where the children sleep.

baby's memories

Start a journal for baby. Include anything you would like. It's fun to do a daily log of the things you do together on the days you spend with each other. In between visits you might include drawings sent from the child or letters sent by his parents. You may want to write poems, describe the daily world news, or relate similar experiences from your own life. Whatever you decide to write will be cherished, and will be a different point of view from what his parents would write!

★ Wit & Wisdom ★

One time when my thirteen-year-old daughter and I were having our usual argument— with her saying I must hate her to give her such stupid rules—I pulled out her journal that I'd been writing in since before she was born. I read a few pages to her aloud. The argument stopped.
—Rebecca, Fairfax, Virginia

excursions

Investigate what is going on for the children in your area. A good resource is the local parenting newspaper, which is usually free and available wherever you find services that cater to children, or call the local library and ask them. Look for live children's theaters, children's museums, farm visits, or local parks. Plan a few things to do in advance and schedule the week accordingly. It's amazing how much easier life goes when you have a plan!

traditions

Decide on special traditions you want to pass on to your grandchildren. These might be activities they may only do with you, like nature walks, nighttime bonfires, special meal menus, afternoon tea, or a special song at bedtime. Think of the traditions you had in your family when you were a child, pass on those old traditions or make up new ones. The important thing is to give your grandchildren experiences they can count on each time they are with you. This builds memories and allows them to feel the family connection.

★ Wit & Wisdom ★

Sometimes when a baby is fussy and cross, I have found these secret words can work miracles. The words have been passed down from one generation to the next. Don't laugh, but the magic words are "tootie...tootie..." Hold the baby tightly and whisper "tootie...tootie..." over and over again in a low voice close to her ear. You will be surprised how soothing this is to her.
—Suzanne R., Indianapolis, Indiana

photo opportunity

Take many photographs of your grandbaby. Go through an entire day cataloguing the simplest things, like waking up, eating breakfast, taking a walk, bath time, or playing. Make sure you are in some, if not all, of the pictures. When you develop the film make two prints, one for you and one for baby. Take the pictures and put them in a small picture album that baby can carry around. Write stick-on notes beneath the photos so that when you are not around someone else can read them to baby, as a reminder of your days together. Put the second set of prints in an album for yourself, never to be touched by gooey hands!

individual attention

When visiting more than one grandchild at a time, make sure to spend individual time with each child. Children notice how much attention baby gets, so make an extra-special effort with the older sibling to assure him of his continued place in your heart! A perfect time for you to create a special space for the older child is when Mom is nursing. Do a project, read a story, make up a puppet show, hug each other, go for a walk. Most important, pay attention to what the child says to you and listen intently. Make sure to get some time alone to hold and bond with baby too.

life on tape

There is so much communicated in a voice. Whether you are an old or young grandparent, you won't be alive forever, so start recording your life story on tape now. It will be a gift your grandchild may not even hear until she is ten years or older, but she will cherish it. Tell parts of your life intertwined with her life, things you do together, impressions of her personality, your feelings and thoughts, the world's differences now from when you were a child, her parents' life adventures, etc. There doesn't have to be any preplanned narration, just talk. Make a few notes to yourself about what areas were mentioned so you won't repeat yourself over the years. Add to your tapes at least once a month.

plant a garden

Plant a small garden together at your house or theirs! Simple vegetables like carrots, cucumbers, tomatoes, sunflowers, and pumpkins grow fast. Draw pictures of what you expect to grow and glue them to thick popsicle sticks. Push the sticks into the ground near the seeds. It might be fun to go to the store, get some grown vegetables like the ones you planted, and make something with them. If the grandchildren will not be visiting when the vegetables arrive, take pictures and send them with a little story about you caring for the garden!

picture frame

Buy one of those large picture frames that has fifteen or twenty small picture spaces. In the spaces, put old pictures of the child's parents at similar ages. You may have fun posing baby in similar positions, then taking pictures of him to be added to the frame near the ones of his parents. Children like to see a resemblance between themselves and their parents. They also find it funny, and a bit hard to believe, that their parents were ever children!

314

★ **Wit & Wisdom** ★

For infants, search out the onesies with the little mitts that pull over baby's hands to prevent them from scratching their face.
—Janet, New York, New York

grandma's jewelry box

Take some time on a rainy afternoon to pull out your old jewelry box (if you don't have one, visit the local thrift store). That big chunky costume jewelry that is no longer in style will light up your grandchild's eyes. Tell her stories about the events like weddings and parties you wore that jewelry to. If you have old pictures, pull those out too. Let the children try things on and look in the mirror. Don't give them all the jewelry at once; it's more fun for them to look forward to the surprises in Grandma's jewelry box.

lullaby lane

Sing lullabies that you remember to grandbaby. If you can't remember any, make one up so it can be passed on. Sing this lullaby every time you hold your grandbaby; other times, simply hum the melody. Baby will begin to recognize this song and feel soothed when she hears it. If you live far away, make a tape of yourself singing a few songs, saying poems or rhymes, or reading stories.

★ Wit & Wisdom ★

With family all over the country, our son only sees some relatives once a year or so. To make sure he knows names and faces, I made a family photo album with a page for each person. Don't worry about it being pretty—use a photocopier that enlarges or a computer scanner and printer and just cut and paste away.
—Sam, Boise, Idaho

childproofing grandparent's house

Taking baby to visit grandparents is a challenge if you arrive unprepared. So, make sure to pack one child gate, ten electric outlet plugs, a roll of thick masking tape, rubber bands, and padded corner guards. Upon arrival to Grandma's house:

- Go through the house and take any cleaning supplies or poisonous products and put them out of reach.
- Scan the kitchen for appliances with cords within reach, move them to the back of counters and use masking tape the cords out of reach.
- Remove tablecloths so kids won't pull any hot food or heavy items on top of themselves.
- Tape a sign to the bathroom mirrors that says, "Keep door closed at all times."
- Move beds and furniture away from the windows.
- Clear bedside tables.
- Move houseplants out of reach.
- Move low tables with sharp corners into closets or attach corner guards.
- Put rubber bands on cabinet handles on all doors that are unsafe for kids to open.
- Masking tape all cords to the wall to make sure they are out of pulling reach.

recording your thoughts

your child's journal

Buy a blank book and start writing to your child today. Your child may not be born or your child may be two years old; whatever the age, it is never too late to begin recording your thoughts, feelings, observations, and descriptions of your child's life and personality. Write as often as you can and include your feelings about your baby, how she contributes to the beauty of your life and most of all your feelings of love. Write letters to her, things you want baby to know when she is an adult, cute things she does that you might forget over time. As your baby grows into adolescence read her some of your thoughts when she is going through a hard time, or when she thinks you hate her because you need to correct a behavior. It will remind her that you have been loving her for a very long time. When your child leaves home, give her this precious journal. This might just be the gift your child will cherish most from you.

Today, we took you for a ride in a wagon around the block. You laughed and smiled the whole time.

no time for problems

Parents are usually too busy to solve problems, they just live through them! Pick a problem in your life. Be brave and take a minute to write down the problem in the middle of a blank sheet of paper. Brainstorm every solution you can think of. Don't let your solutions be judged by whether or not they seem possible at this time. Your brainstorming solutions are like seeds planted in a field—one will take root over time and begin to grow. Feeling and expressing the problem will make you feel better, even if no immediate solution is at hand.

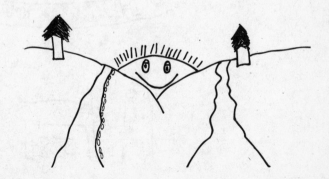

birthday letter

Write a birthday letter to your baby every year. It doesn't matter if you have missed one, two, or five. What will matter is that on baby's eighteenth birthday you can hand her letters that have been written about her life, as a baby, young girl, teenager and on. They will be a living example of how much you loved, supported, and encouraged her. So often as parents we think we will remember everything, but we don't. Make sure to read them over, and make copies before you give them away.

news update

Whenever a major news event occurs, take a picture of your baby holding that newspaper or magazine. Make sure the heading of the day can be seen clearly. Keep all of these pictures in a special photo album, continuing to add to it as baby grows up. As children begin to learn U.S. history in school, they may ask you where they were or how old they were when something important happened. You'll be able to show them the photos. Attach a large envelope to the back of the photo album. Save the front page of the paper or magazine, fold it up and stick it in the envelope. History is much more relevant, exciting, and fun when it relates directly to us.

positive feelings

Materials
Index cards
Pen

Do you ever feel tired, as though you don't want to get out of bed? Or maybe you feel sad about some aspect of your life. On the index cards write down positive, happy, uplifting thoughts of your own, or quotes by others. When you wake up in the morning, read them. Before you go to bed at night, read them again. When you feel tired or sad, read them. It helps to write down positive affirmations in the areas of your life that are a challenge for you. It's a way of retraining your brain. For example, if you are not a morning person and you dislike getting out of bed in the morning, the affirmation might read "I will wake up bright and ready to face the morning with energy and happiness." It's possible this could be called brainwashing, but at least it is self-brainwashing and it works!

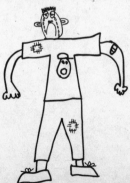

what's in a name?

When your baby grows up to be five or six years old, he will definitely want to know why you chose the name you did for him, what other names you thought of, and why you didn't choose one of those names. So keep one step ahead of them and write it down! Write the list of names and your thoughts on each one. Most important, write your baby's chosen name with as much information as you can find: what the name means, country of origin, etc. If baby is named after someone, include personal information on that person.

fantasy day

New parents have little time for leisure, so here's a way to sneak a fantasy day into thirty minutes! First, write down your fantasy day in detail from morning to night. Everything must go the way YOU want it to. Maybe you wake up in the morning to a day with nothing to do but read. Do you spend the day scuba diving from a beautiful yacht? Do you envision yourself lounging on a tropical island? Is your fantasy a day when everyone in your life treats you like a queen? Hope and dream big, and remember, this is a fantasy! When you finish writing, close your eyes and visualize in clear detail yourself going through your fantasy day.

your journal

Writing thoughts and feelings down in a special book that only you read is called journalizing. It is amazing what pearls of insight can be gained by this simple reflection. Buy a blank book today and begin writing. When you look back every few months, growth will be obvious! Write everything you think, fear, dream, or wonder. If you need to make a decision, write about it—your own advice will surprise you.

★ Wit & Wisdom ★

We live in an apartment, so we can't make marks on the wall as our daughter grows, so we decided to paint a cloth wall-hanging to look like a tree. We each put our hands in paint and then pressed them to the cloth to create the leaves. The trunk of the tree is the ruler for recording her growth. Best of all, we can take it with us wherever we go.
—Diane E., Cupertino, California

letter to yourself

Sometimes when moms and dads get caught up in daily duties like caregiving and work they lose sight of the larger picture of their lives. Seeing the larger picture means being able to see the present day as part of a whole lifetime. Take a few minutes today and write a letter. The letter will be from your twenty-year-old child written to you. Start the letter like this:

Dear Mom and Dad,
I learned so many things from you about life...
During the hardest parts of my life you...
When I didn't know what decisions to make...

Add whatever you want to this letter, date it, and keep it. Shaping and guiding a child is a life's work that merely starts with how you talk to baby on the changing table. What you do, say, and model to your child creates a life. In other words, what you are doing is important work. Remember that the next time you wake up at 4 a.m. to feed or soothe your little darling!

life story

We all have a story to tell. What better time than the present to write down on paper the memories you have of your life. As you watch your children go through similar experiences, you'll be reminded of your own childhood. Also, parents and relatives will be more likely to tell you stories about yourself after you have your own children, whether you ask for the stories or not. You don't have to be a great writer to write your life story. All you need to do is try to remember, and be as honest as possible with your feelings. In fact, as baby grows, these stories from your life will make great bedtime stories; you can even make them seem more dramatic, your part more heroic, your struggle illuminating important life choices. Here is your chance to be the star.

daydream

In your journal or on a blank sheet of paper, begin to write the dreams you have for your life. Write everything you can think of, no matter how out of reach it may seem. You may want to divide the page into categories: personal, children, marriage, career, and material possessions. The important thing is not to restrict your dream writing in any way. Do this every few months and compare your reality to what you've written. You may also start a dream file. This is a more visual way of dreaming. You cut pictures out of magazines that represent what you are trying to create. Date them and put them in a file folder. Take the folder out once in a while to check how many of your dreams you've been able to create. Don't be surprised if dreams come true—vision is a strong motivator.

★ Wit & Wisdom ★

Someone once told me something when I was thinking of going back to college to get a master's degree. She said that I should first write down what I wanted out of my life, then decide if I needed a master's degree to achieve it. That person saved me years of education I didn't need.
—Angela M., Hartford, Connecticut

letter of thanks

Throughout your life, there have been people who have guided, sup-ported, loved, encouraged, and lead you. Take time today to think of someone from your childhood who helped shape you into the parent you are. Remember what qualities he or she had. Write a letter telling about yourself today, about your family, about the goals and dreams you have accomplished, and most important, what you learned by watching him or her. It's so important to support the positive in our world; so often, we remember the hurt, but forget the positive. Tell this person you found a hero in them.

make a family tree

Family trees are fun to draw. It gives children a sense of where every-one fits in and it makes them feel a part of something bigger than their immediate family. A good way to do a family tree is to give children pieces of paper for them to decorate that represent women and men. Cut out circles for women and squares for men, and have children dec-orate them and name them. Once all family members and relatives have a piece of paper with their name on it, start gluing the circles and squares to a large piece of paper. Talk about family members as you glue them to the paper. If you have no idea what a family tree looks like, go to the library and look for a reference book.

write a family newsletter

Plan to write a newsletter after your family's next vacation, or begin the tradition of writing a newsletter once a year to catch everyone up on the family's adventures. Anyone who wants to can be a reporter looking for a story. Obviously baby is too young to participate in the writing of these newsletters, so make sure to keep a copy of each and put it in his memory box. Older brothers and sisters might need an assistant to dictate their story to. Although your vacation or adventures may include the majesty of Mt. Everest or the magnificence of the Grand Canyon, your most inspired article might be about the anthill at your picnic, or the outrageous waitress that one night at dinner. It is as much fun planning what you'll include in your newsletter as creating it. Don't forget to include drawings. Once written, print it up and send it out to friends and relatives. They'll love hearing about all the family's news, stories, and adventures.

make a timeline

Make a family timeline by taping several sheets of paper end to end. Draw a line though the middle of the entire length. At the left end, make a short vertical line through the timeline and date it with the year the family started. Mark each twelve-inch interval along the timeline with a vertical line, each one dated one year later. Take it one year at a time, with everyone contributing everything they can remember. Write it down on the timeline. Keep working on this until you reach the current date. Hang it up on a wall as a reminder of what your family has already accomplished and experienced together.

games parents play

new baby survival

- Sleep is your number one priority. Everyone is going to tell you to sleep when the baby sleeps. What they won't tell you is that means you will get absolutely nothing else done. Let that be OK for the first few months.
- Even if you are a new parent, there is within you a wellspring of intuitive knowing. Go with your gut. Advice may be coming at you from all angles, remember they don't really have any better idea than you do!
- If someone asks if you need help—say YES! Don't overlook baby's dad as a great source of help. Let him take care of baby alone from the beginning—he will bond with baby as he figures out what to do. You may want to pick a certain part of baby's day, like bathtime or bedtime, and let dad be in charge.
- Get out of the house with or without baby. Join a mothers group, a playgroup, get someone to baby-sit so you can meet a friend, go out on a date with your spouse, or attend a class.
- Enjoy the time you have with your baby. Life with a new baby may be very different than what you thought it would be, most likely it is harder but also more joy-filled than you ever expected. Take your attention off the mechanics of doing everything right, having a clean house, or producing eatable food—and relax into baby's world.

balancing the workload

The concept of equal parenting is gaining much acclaim with today's parents. How do you take the new roles and responsibilities that come with having a new baby and divide them so that neither parent gets worn out, resents the other, or becomes bogged down with duties?

Set aside a weekly time to go over how each person is contributing to baby care and household responsibilities. If there is a problem or someone feels the load isn't being carried by both parents, suggest ways that the inequality can be dealt with.

Set up your weekly schedule. The primary baby care person needs a break by the end of the day and is most likely looking forward to a spouse's return from work. If a meeting or extracurricular activity is planned, make sure it is on the calendar.

Don't assume that mom is better than dad at nurturing baby. If dad has a chance from the beginning to have bonding time alone with baby, he is just as capable as soothing baby, feeding her, putting her to sleep, changing diapers, and carrying her around while he does chores.

Make sure to leave time for the two of you as a couple. It may seem that baby has taken over your world, and that may be the case—but it will be the time you dedicate to your relationship that will keep you sane.

diaper rash

Diaper rash is caused by the combination of high moisture, little air, chemical irritants, and infectious organisms found in urine and feces, together with the rubbing of diapers or clothing on tender skin. Diaper rash usually peaks between the seventh and ninth months, when a more varied diet is introduced. After a while, baby's skin toughens up. Here are a few preventative steps.

- Change baby often, once an hour when baby is awake, or at least before or after every feeding and whenever there is a bowel movement.
- Give baby's bottom more air. Try keeping baby's bottom bare part of the day. Place cloth diapers or a doubled receiving blanket or waterproof pad underneath her. If she's wearing disposable diapers, poke a few holes in the waterproof outer cover to give her more air.
- Don't dry out baby's skin with frequent washes with soap or wipes. Use warm water and cotton balls if baby has had a bowel movement. Don't use baby wipes at all when baby has a rash. If baby is merely wet, just change diaper.
- Spread a thick, protective layer of ointment (A&D, Desitin, zinc oxide, Eucerin, Nivia). Use these liberally, but don't use the ointment when airing baby's bottom. Do not use talc on rash.
- If rash doesn't clear up in a day or two, or if blisters of pustules appear, call the doctor.

ways to soothe crying

When baby starts to cry, parents generally run through a list of possible causes, the most immediate being hunger or a dirty diaper. But there are other more subtle things that baby might be communicating.

- Baby might have been startled by a loud noise, a bright light, or unfamiliar smell. Some babies have trouble with the sensory input from the world around them. If your baby seems to be hypersensitive, try to reduce sources of stimulation in your home, turn down the volume, close the drapes, and build more quiet peaceful time into your day.
- Babies can easily become overstimulated. If baby's had a long day, many visitors, or a stressful outing, crying may be the only option to empty their sensory overload. Afterwards, baby will seem wide awake and peaceful or fall fast asleep. Hold baby as he cries, talking softly as you act relaxed.
- Clothes, diapers, toys may have pinched or bothered baby. The littlest annoyances can bring on screams. If nothing else seems to be wrong, undress baby and look to see if his body has any red marks from clothes that might be too tight, or a place he might have scratched himself. Let him lie naked for awhile.
- Constipation is another cause for wailing. If baby has hard, pelletlike poops and he's over two months old, give him a little prune juice.
- Colic is another culprit. Nobody really knows what causes it, but baby will react by pulling her legs up towards her chest and twisting. Try holding baby in a football hold, massaging baby's stomach or turning on an air-conditioner or vacuum cleaner so the crying doesn't seem as loud. Colic can continue for two to three months. Consult your doctor if you have fears it might be something else.
- After looking for medical causes, the best you can do is to act relaxed, try to be soothing by rocking, singing, or holding, and then gradually teach baby how to soothe herself.

thumb and pacifier tips

Baby's mouth is important for exploration and pleasure as well as eating. Most babies will suck on something, either their fingers or a pacifier, at some time during the first year of life. Let baby enjoy the comfort and satisfaction he receives from sucking.

Pacifier

- Make sure that breast-feeding is well established before introducing a pacifier, and don't offer baby a pacifier when he's hungry.
- Limit pacifier use to between feedings. Hungry babies might be satisfied with the pacifier and forget to eat.
- Don't dip a pacifier into a sweetened liquid, it could lead to cavities.
- Throw a pacifier out after two or three months. Bacteria builds up and you wouldn't want a worn plastic nipple to wear off in baby's mouth.
- Never attach a cord or ribbon to a pacifier.

Thumb

- There is no evidence that thumb sucking is a sign of emotional illness, nor does it do damage to the permanent teeth if the thumb sucking ceases by age five.
- Attempts to wean a child from the thumb do not need to begin until age four.
- If breast-fed, make sure the thumb sucking isn't a substitute for time baby would like to be sucking at the breast.
- If thumb sucking seems to take away from normal exploration or play time, occasionally remove thumb from baby's mouth and try to distract with a game.

good night, baby!

Establish good sleeping habits early. Teach baby how to fall asleep on her own by putting her in the crib while she's still awake. Babies wake up many times during the night, so those who know how to soothe themselves back to sleep get a better night's rest.

- Develop nighttime rituals and patterns that baby can count on. Doing the same thing each night creates structure and helps baby to anticipate what will be coming next—sleep!
- During the nighttime ritual, give yourself at least 30 minutes of calming down time, bathing, reading books, massage, singing songs, so that baby will be ready for sleep.
- Limit stimulating activities or watching TV for at least two hours before bedtime and don't let baby take a nap late in the day.
- Make baby's room and crib an appealing place. Have a night light or bed-side lamp available if baby prefers a little light. Decide on a special toy or blanket that is not allowed to leave baby's room. Play soothing music while baby falls asleep. Put a heating pad on baby's bed a half hour before she goes to sleep so that her bed is warm and cozy.
- Create a personalized sleep book. Take pictures of him sleeping in various places around the house, in the car, or in the stroller. When it is naptime or bedtime, look through the picture book together.

ear infection prevention

- Breast-feed for at least three months, this helps baby build immunity against ear infections.
- Feed baby upright. In babies, the ear's eustachian tube goes in a straight line from the mouth to the nose to the ear. When baby lies flat, the formula or milk may drain into the middle ear.
- Don't smoke. Babies exposed to secondhand smoke get more ear infections because the smoke irritates the mucous membranes and damages tiny hairs in the middle ear.
- Elevate baby's sleeping position when he has a cold. Be sure to put the pillows under the head of the mattress, not under baby's head.
- Give baby a decongestant when he has a cold, especially before an airplane flight. Have baby suck on breast or bottle during take-off and landing.
- Home-based child care, rather than group day care, tends to have less infectious illnesses, so if baby has repeated ear infections this might be a consideration.

stranger anxiety

Between six and nine months, babies may develop a preference for those who care for them on a daily basis. Although it might feel troubling when baby refuses to be held by others, this is a good sign of social maturity. This fear of strangers may disappear quickly or not show up at all. If baby is afraid, don't force her to be sociable. Instead do the following:

- Warn friends and family that baby is going through a fearful stage and that they shouldn't try to pick her up immediately. Instead, they should smile at her, offer her a toy, talk to her quietly, or do other interactive play without touching or reaching out for her.
- Allow baby to sit on your lap or near you when others are in the room.
- Let baby get to know a caregiver before leaving them alone. If you need to leave him with a new caregiver during this fearful stage make sure to schedule enough time before you leave the house for the caregiver to slowly approach baby and interact with him while you are in the room.
- Don't sneak away. During this stage it is likely that baby will be crying when you leave. Even if it looks like baby is engaged in play with the caregiver, don't leave without saying good-bye, otherwise baby will feel he can't depend on you and may become more clingy.
- Don't let this worry you. Stranger anxiety comes and goes all the way up to eighteen months old. Be patient, try to give your baby the security he needs, and let him set his own pace in accepting and interacting with strangers.

introducing solids

Most babies are ready at six months to begin eating solids. At that time he'll have lost the tongue-thrust reflex that makes baby push anything that isn't liquid out of his mouth, and his stomach will be ready to digest a wider range of food.

- First time: Let baby nurse or have a bottle for a few minutes so that he's not so hungry that he'll be too fussy to eat. Make sure there aren't too many distractions. For the first bite, try very thin rice cereal. Mix one teaspoon of cereal with four teaspoons of breast milk, formula, or water. Put about 1/4 of a teaspoon on the spoon, place it between baby's lips, and see what happens!
- Don't worry if baby isn't interested at first. Continue offering baby cereal the next day. If she refuses a few days in a row, put the cereal away for a week and then try again.
- Once baby is eating, keep offering her cereal two or three times a day. You can then begin adding barley or oatmeal cereal and pureed fruits and vegetables. Make sure to add only one new item every three days to make sure baby doesn't have an allergic reaction (a rash, diarrhea, or vomiting).
- Baby knows how much food he needs. When he stops eating, take the food away. During growth spurts he may eat much more than usual.
- It is a myth that solids help babies sleep through the night. The truth is that babies wake naturally in the middle of the night, they just haven't learned how to soothe themselves back to sleep.

doctor-parent relationship

It is important to have an open, communicative, and trusting relationship with your baby's doctor. Here's how:

- Keep a Doctor Diary. Buy a pocket-size notebook to use at home. Jot down each question you have as it comes up so you won't forget about it when you get to your appointment. If you think your baby might be coming down with a cold, note the symptoms you notice so you can describe them easily. During your appointment, use the diary to take notes. If the illness is a recurring one you will want to write in the diary how effective the treatment or medication was.
- Schedule appointments when both you and the doctor will not feel rushed. When scheduling your appointment, ask when the doctor is least busy, morning in the middle of the week are usually best.
- Tell your doctor the truth. Withholding facts, even if they embarrass you, may lead to a misdiagnosis or unnecessary treatment. If your baby spits the prescribed medicine out, make sure you call and tell him or her the problems you're having, he or she may have helpful solutions you haven't thought of.
- Ask questions and get clarification if there is anything the doctor says that you don't understand.
- If you aren't sure if you agree with a doctor's diagnosis be sure to ask for referrals. Even when you do trust your doctor, it is smart to get a second opinion when you feel it is necessary.
- Get to know the nurse. In most offices, the nurse will be calling you back to find out what is happening with your baby. Be prepared to tell her and have your schedule at hand so you can quickly agree to an appointment time.

parental confidence

Today's parents are lucky to have so much information at their finger-tips. However, all the information can be confusing and lead some parents to doubt their own intuitive ideas, knowledge, and long-held thoughts of how they would like to parent. Books, articles, and even the experts disagree and contradict each other on many points. Twenty years ago there was one theory on nursing and discipline, now there is a completely different one. Yet, all the children raised with the old theory turned out fine, just as your baby will grow up and know how to walk, talk, eat, potty, and have friends, even if he doesn't meet all the projected milestones. The most important gift you have to give your children is not the knowledge you seek so that you can be the perfect parent—it is the time you spend in the moment, loving them. Keep turning inward and trust that you have the best answers.

the question of television

Television viewing has many drawbacks and very few redeeming qualities. Statistics show that children two to twelve years old in the U.S. watch an average of twenty-five hours of TV a week. By the time they graduate from high school, they will have spent more time watching TV than they have spent in school! They will have seen 350,000 commercials, 18,000 murders, as well as thousands of sexual encounters. TV viewing is also linked to obesity and poor school performance, and it interferes with family life as well as confusing a child's value system. So what is a parent to do?

- If you do decide to let your baby watch TV, wait until he reaches a stage where he is actually excited about the show (somewhere around 12 months). Then pick a one-hour non-commercial show whose message you agree with.
- Limit the rest of the family's TV viewing during hours when baby is awake. Parents who depend on TV as their main form of nightly entertainment will create children with the same habits.
- Resist the temptation to use the TV as a baby-sitter and instead watch the show with your child pointing out familiar objects. Use the show as an opportunity to discuss topics of interest discussed on the show.

★ Wit & Wisdom ★

Six years ago I took the TV out of my house. My kids were furious. A year later the twelve- and thirteen-year-old thanked me, saying that without the temptation to watch they actually had more fun with their friends and got better grades—it is the best parenting decision I've ever made.
—Sam W., Tucson, Arizona

bottle weaning

Most pediatricians recommend bottle weaning around a year old. Even though the bottle is a great source of emotional comfort and gratification, there are many reasons to wean your baby at this age.

- Threat to baby's baby teeth and the permanent ones yet to come.
- May interfere with good eating habits. If baby sucks on a bottle of milk or juice all day long it may suppress feelings of hunger.
- Baby might be more likely to suffer ear infections.
- Development might be delayed as baby crawls or walks around all day with a bottle in her hand—it means she only has one hand available to play or explore.

How to separate baby from bottle:

- Reduce bottle feedings slowly. Start by replacing a midday bottle with a sippy cup or straw (see From Bottle to Straw).
- Limit when, where, and how often baby has a bottle.
- Don't allow baby to walk, crawl, or suck on it as he plays. Have baby sit in your lap or in the high chair when he drinks from it.
- Fill the bottle with water only—this may reduce baby's interest.
- Set a rule that the bottle cannot leave the house.
- At bedtime, only let baby suck on his bottle before brushing his teeth, then tuck him in without the bottle.
- Weaning baby from his bottle may take many months, so be patient.

biting

Baby may want to test his new set of teeth. At first the biting is playful and experimental, and baby has no idea that he's hurting someone. Here's what to do if you want it to stop.

- Don't overreact, baby would be delighted with a high-pitched scream.
- Look her in the eye and say, "No biting," as sternly as you can.
- Divert baby's attention with a song, toy, or other distraction
- Do not bite the child back to show him what it feels like.
- Think through the activities leading up to the bite. If baby was roughhousing with an older sibling, trying to get a toy he wanted, or felt he was threatened, baby might have bitten as a way of expressing that he wanted the behavior to stop.

the question of discipline

Discipline is not really something you do to baby, rather it is a way of behaving with your child. The word *discipline* actually comes from the Latin word for teaching. Here are a few discipline pointers.

- Until baby understands what is safe and what is not, parents have total responsibility for keeping the environment safe.
- Connect with your baby by looking eye to eye before saying anything.
- Personalize your response by using baby's name. Instead of simply saying, "No," or "Don't do that!" try saying "Not Peter's toy."
- Make your response short and sweet using as few words as possible to make your point.
- Use the trick of substituting what you want her to do and distracting her from what she was doing. For example, instead of "No, you can't play with Mommy's glasses," try "Play with these plastic keys."
- Give baby choices instead of demanding she do something, but make sure that no matter what choice she makes, baby will be doing what you want her to do. Instead of saying, "Put your toys away," you might try, "Do you want to put the dolls or blocks away first?"
- Instead of using the suggestion, "If you do this, then ____," which suggests your child has a choice, say "When you do this, then you can do that."

avoiding conflict

Around fifteen months, babies know what they want and they can be very loud in forcing you to give it to them. Here are a few ways to avoid or deal with possible problems.

- Anticipate the problem. Try to avoid situations where you know your child is likely to misbehave. If baby hates to sit in grocery store carts, wiggles, reaches for food, cries, and makes your trip miserable—don't take her. If you know she screams for candy at the checkout, distract her with how the scanner works, or pull a small toy out of your purse.
- Go over the day's schedule in advance, giving baby an idea of what will happen and in what order.
- Let your child have some control over the day. Even if it is just thirty minutes, set aside time every day for her to be in charge of the activity.
- Stay calm when your child loses it. Don't get rattled by the loud screams, and keep your voice slow and reassuring while you tell her that you know she's upset. The goal is to help her calm down.
- Leave if you have to. Removing her from the problem situation allows you a chance to sit with baby, calm down, and then talk about why a rule, or whatever conflict caused the eruption, exists.

that isn't fair

When a new baby joins the family, it is the beginning of parents hearing the words, "That isn't fair, "Why does baby get to do that?" or "Why can't I do this?" In their desire to prevent sibling fighting, many parents strive to make things fair. This isn't always possible since kids aren't the same, so it is impossible to always treat them the same way. Here are some tips to avoid fights or hurt feelings when things can't be fair.

- Focus on age, ability, and specific needs of each child. Divide responsibilities and privileges, according to age. Baby might get to be held more than an older child because he needs to be held to be fed, whereas an older child may get more play time with a parent because of his age and ability to play.
- Don't try to be equal, but do keep track of how much attention you give each child. If on one day one child needs more from you, try to even it out the next with time given to the other.
- Do things together when you don't have enough time to give each child equal attention. If you are going to read a story, include both kids but read two books, one for each child.
- Make sure to express extra love and attention to older children. When baby appears on the scene, jealousy is inevitable. So if you are looking to make things more equal, tip the scale in favor of the sibling.

quieting fears

There are many things in baby's everyday world that may cause him to be afraid. Although they may seem silly to you, they are very real to baby. A barking dog, the blender, the dark, a neighbor's motorcycle, taking a bath, or even a vacuum cleaner could be the source of great fear for him. Here's what to do if your baby has a fear.

- Don't force baby to face the fear. Holding baby as he cries, while you lean over reassuring him that the neighbor's dog (who is as big as a horse is to us) is friendly and will not bite him, is not going to make baby less afraid of dogs, and in fact may intensify the fear.
- Don't make fun of your child's fears by calling them silly. Baby's fears are very serious to him. If you take them seriously, baby will feel validated and be willing to learn to deal with them.
- Accept baby's fears as real and comfort him accordingly. If baby screams when you turn on the blender, be quick to pick him up and reassure him. Just don't overdo your response or baby might think there truly is something to be afraid of.
- Your long-term goal is to help him overcome his fears. Start slowly by allowing him to approach the feared item at his own pace, one step at a time. Let him touch or play with appliances he fears while they are turned off and unplugged. If he's afraid of the bathtub, let him sit with his toys in the bath with no water until he feels the bathtub is a friendly place. Once he masters the first steps, slowly move toward introducing the next. Turn on the appliance while you hold him, or ask your neighbor to play with his dog at a distance while you hold baby and look on. Then the next day, stand closer as the neighbor plays with the dog until you can stand right next to the dog.

clothing wars

Around eighteen months, baby begins to show her personality. She wants to choose which clothes to wear. A tutu in the middle of winter is no problem for her, or perhaps two different shoes, even dress-up clothes that drag as she walks are an option when going to a family event. Here's how to avoid clothing wars.

- Arrange her clothing so that outfits are matched and set out together; this way, if she wants to choose her clothing, she'll pick an already matched outfit.
- If baby receives "dress-up" clothes (make-believe stuff) set a rule from the beginning that these clothing items are for play and not to be worn outside the house (unless of course, you don't mind!).
- Remember that originality is a good thing. If you can set your own feelings aside and stop worrying what others might think when they see your child dressed in mismatched frocks, you will not have clothing wars.

★ Wit & Wisdom ★

When my daughter was two she used to wear two different shoes each day. She thought it was a lot of fun to not match. She was still doing this at five. The funny thing was that some of the other girls thought it was cool and they started doing it too. My daughter is now sixteen years old and she's reminded me more than once how much she appreciates the fact that I've always encouraged her to be herself, no matter what it looked like to others.
—Nancy B., Hendersonville, Tennessee

moving to a bed

When baby is more than thirty-six inches tall or seems to have figured out how to crawl out of his crib, he is ready to move into a bed.

- Make sure the room is child-proofed since it is likely he may also get out of his bed. Put a gait across the door or keep his door closed so he won't be able to wander around the house.
- Use a guardrail in the beginning, or buy a padded bed surround so he won't fall out onto the floor.
- Include him in the purchase of the new bed, new sheets, and blanket of his choosing.

Make a big occasion the night he moves to the new bed, perhaps giving him a new stuffed animal, talking about the "big-boy" bed.

development

the first two months, big and small muscles

Things babies will do with big muscles:

- lift head for a moment or two
- search for something to suck
- hold on when falling
- turn head if breathing is obstructed
- does not control arm and leg movements

Things babies will do with small muscles:

- clench fists
- hold whatever is placed in their hands
- stare at objects
- stare at faces
- avoid brightness
- begin to coordinate eyes

Some other things babies do at this stage are eat frequently, wet a lot, hiccup, sneeze, sleep, yawn, and make interesting noises.

the first two months, express and think

Things babies will do to express themselves and learn about the world:

- cry
- might smile
- respond to being held
- become calmed by faces
- make eye contact
- believe they are the world, not separate from it

Things babies will do that show they're thinking:

- eyes follow faces and things as they move
- suck and chew things near their mouths
- listen

three to five months, big and small muscles

Things babies will do with big muscles:

- begin to control arms and legs
- lift and control head better when held upright
- kick their feet

Things babies will do with small muscles:

- hands still fisted, but relaxed some of the time
- arms reach for things with hands fisted as they swing and miss

Other things baby might do at this stage include sucking their fists and pulling your hair and ears!

three to five months, express and think

Things babies will do to express themselves and learn about the world:

- use voice to express a variety of feelings
- realize hands and feet are part of their own bodies
- explore face with hands
- recognize you and other family members
- babble when talked to

Things babies will do that show they're thinking:

- look longer at things
- look from one thing to another
- hold object and move it around
- look for source of noises they hear
- cry less
- babble, coo, and gurgle to themselves and others

six to eight months, big and small muscles

Things babies will do with big muscles:

- roll from place to place
- move from back to stomach and back again
- have better head control
- creep forward and backward
- get to sitting position by rolling over

Things babies will do with small muscles:

- reach with one arm
- grab things within reach
- use thumb and forefinger in pincer grasp
- move things from hand to hand

six to eight months, express and think

Things babies will do to express themselves and learn about the world:

- display a greater variety of feelings
- be more aware of body parts
- hear name and respond
- begin to see self as separate from the world
- prefer certain tastes to others
- want to feed self
- not welcome strange faces
- call out for help

Things babies will do that show they're thinking:

- develop greater memory
- be alert during waking hours
- pick up object, then drop it and look for it
- imitate others' vocal tones and inflection patterns
- use more sounds to express feelings
- see and grab for things they want

nine to eleven months, big and small muscles

Things babies will do with big muscles:

- crawl
- crawl with stiff legs
- crawl while holding something
- use furniture to pull self upright
- stand without help
- get stuck in standing position, unable to get down
- cruise along by holding onto furniture
- sit up alone

Things babies will do with small muscles:

- use thumb and forefinger to pick up small things
- use forefinger to point, touch, and poke

nine to eleven months, express and think

Things babies will do to express themselves and learn about the world:

- fear separation
- grow very attached to important people in their lives
- feed self
- drink from cup
- gain more interest in what's going on around them
- anticipate actions and activities

Things babies will do that show they're thinking:

- remember things and events from yesterday
- be able to concentrate
- want to know "what happens if...?"
- enjoy emptying and refilling
- listen to conversations

twelve to seventeen months, big and small muscles

Things babies will do with big muscles:

- stand without holding onto anything
- walk
- prefer to crawl sometimes
- climb up and down stairs
- might climb out of crib

Things babies will do with small muscles:

- undress self
- untie shoes
- use one hand more than the other

twelve to seventeen months, express and think

Things babies will do to express themselves and learn about the world:

- show many emotions
- be fearful of strangers and unfamiliar places
- begin to know what is theirs and what isn't
- show affection
- respond to others' feelings
- want to cooperate, but not always
- become better at feeding self
- be able to help dress self
- follow simple requests

Things babies will do that show they're thinking:

- find things that have been hidden
- imitate people
- explore different ways to solve problems
- use trial and error to figure things out
- be able to remember more
- realize words stand for things
- be able to say two to eight words
- use physical gestures to communicate

the road ahead:
eighteen to twenty-four months, big and small muscles

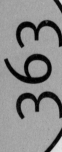

Things babies will do with big muscles:

- walk well
- walk fast
- fall less
- walk up stairs with help
- run, but not smoothly yet

Things babies will do with small muscles:

- feed themselves more successfully
- scribble with crayons or markers
- may untie shoelaces and unzip zippers

the road ahead:
eighteen to twenty-four months, express and think

Things babies will do to express themselves and learn about the world:

- pretend with adult, role-play
- imitate what adult does
- enjoy doing "work" around the house
- have some bladder and bowel control
- desire to dress and undress themselves

Things babies will do that show they're thinking:

- think problems through before taking action
- use more and more words
- use words to get attention and say what they need (they need and want lots of attention)

the road ahead:
the terrific twos

Things babies will do with their muscles:

- run smoothly, though still working on stopping and turning
- throw and kick a ball
- turn pages of a book
- hold eating and drinking utensils
- spill less
- put on easy clothes
- use a paintbrush—with lots of drips

Things babies will do to express themselves:

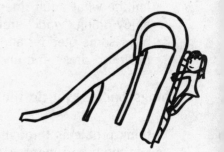

- be very proud of things accomplished
- say "no" even when they mean "yes"
- strive for independence—"me do it"
- try to understand "mine" and "yours"
- name some parts of the body
- narrate what they are doing as they do it
- refer to themselves using their name
- speak two- and three-word sentences
- use "I," "me," and "you," but not always correctly

special thanks

Special thanks to Robin Toews and her artistic fourth graders at Ormondale School in Portola Valley, California, and to Ardath Kroner and her creative second graders at St. Dominics in Benicia, California.

about the authors

Sheila Ellison is the dedicated mother of four children, ages eighteen, seventeen, fourteen, and twelve, and the stepmother of two, ages seventeen and thirteen. She is the creator and author of the 365 series of books, including, *365 Days of Creative Play*, *365 Afterschool Activities*, *365 Foods Kids Love to Eat*, and *365 Ways to Raise Great Kids*. She has appeared on *Oprah*, *The Later Today Show*, and the CBS *Early Show*. Her books have been featured in *O Magazine*, *Parenting*, *Family Circle*, *Glamour*, *Complete Woman*, *Healthy Kids Magazine*, *New York Daily News*, and the *San Francisco Chronicle*, and have been selections of the Children's Book-of-the-Month Club. Sheila has appeared on hundreds of radio shows across the country. She continues to write and live in Northern California.

Susan Ferdinandi has been a preschool teacher for nine years. She is currently working with special needs children. Susan holds a Bachelor of Arts degree from the University of Minnesota and is a member of the National Association for the Education of Young Children. She is the mother of two children, ages fourteen and twelve, and believes that caring for, playing with, and observing her children is her life's most important work.

Notes

_____

_____

_____

_____

_____

_____

_____

_____

_____

_____

_____

_____

_____

Notes

Notes

Notes

Notes

Notes

Notes

_____

_____

_____

_____

_____

_____

_____

_____

_____

_____

_____

_____

Notes

_____

_____

_____

_____

_____

_____

_____

_____

_____

_____

_____

_____